Humanitarian Business

Humanitarian Business

Thomas G. Weiss

polity

First published in 2013 by Polity Press

Polity Press
65 Bridge Street
Cambridge CB2 1UR, UK

Polity Press
350 Main Street
Malden, MA 02148, USA

ISBN-13: 978-0-7456-6331-9
ISBN-13: 978-0-7456-6332-6(pb)

A catalogue record for this book is available from the British Library.

Typeset in 10.25 on 13 pt Scala
by Servis Filmsetting Ltd, Stockport, Cheshire
Printed and bound in Great Britain by the MPG Books Group

For further information on Polity, visit our website: www.politybooks.com

Contents

Figures

Abbreviations

CAP	Consolidated Appeals Process
CERF	Central Emergency Response Fund
DAC	Development Assistance Committee
DHA	Department of Humanitarian Affairs
DPKO	Department of Peacekeeping Operations
DRC	Democratic Republic of the Congo
ECHO	European Community Humanitarian Office
FAO	Food and Agriculture Organization
FTS	Financial Tracking System
ICISS	International Commission on Intervention and State Sovereignty
ICJ	International Court of Justice
ICRC	International Committee of the Red Cross
ICVA	International Council for Voluntary Action
IDP	internally displaced person
IGO	intergovernmental organization
IMF	International Monetary Fund
MSF	Médecins sans Frontières
NATO	North Atlantic Treaty Organization
NGO	nongovernmental organization
NSA	nonstate actor
OCHA	Office for the Coordination of Humanitarian Affairs
ODA	official development assistance
OECD	Organization for Economic Co-operation and Development

PMSCs	private military and security companies
R2P	responsibility to protect
TNC	transnational corporation
UNDP	UN Development Programme
UNDRO	UN Disaster Relief Organization
UNHCR	UN High Commissioner for Refugees
UNICEF	UN Children's Fund
UNRRA	UN Relief and Rehabilitation Administration
UNWRA	UN Relief and Works Agency
USAID	US Agency for International Development
VOICE	Voluntary Organizations Cooperating in Emergencies
WFP	World Food Programme

About the Author

Thomas G. Weiss is Presidential Professor of Political Science at The City University of New York Graduate Center and Director of the Ralph Bunche Institute for International Studies. He directed the United Nations Intellectual History Project (1999–2010) and was President of the International Studies Association (2009–10), Chair of the Academic Council on the UN System (2006–9), editor of *Global Governance*, Research Director of the International Commission on Intervention and State Sovereignty, Research Professor at Brown University's Watson Institute for International Studies, Executive Director of the Academic Council on the UN System and of the International Peace Academy, a member of the UN secretariat, and a consultant to several public and private agencies. He has authored or edited some 45 books and 200 articles and book chapters about multilateral approaches to international peace and security, humanitarian action, and sustainable development. His recent authored volumes include: *Global Governance: Why? What? Whither?* (Polity, 2013); *What's Wrong with the United Nations and How to Fix It*, 2nd edn (Polity Press, 2012); *Humanitarian Intervention: Ideas in Action*, 2nd edn (Polity Press, 2012); *Thinking about Global Governance: Why People and Ideas Matter* (Routledge, 2011); *Humanitarianism Contested: Where Angels Fear to Tread* (Routledge, 2011, with Michael Barnett); *Global Governance and the UN: An Unfinished Journey* (Indiana University Press, 2010, with

Ramesh Thakur); and *UN Ideas That Changed the World* (Indiana University Press, 2009, with Richard Jolly and Louis Emmerij).

Foreword

Thomas G. Weiss has made an outstanding contribution to the understanding and policymaking of humanitarian action for more than twenty-five years. In this new book, he continues to do so by challenging international humanitarians and their government donors to think about their profession as a business.

To approach humanitarian action as a commercial proposition is – as Weiss notes early on – deeply scandalous to the majority of people who see it as a healing profession based on values, rights, and needs. Most people become humanitarians or give to humanitarian agencies because they care about the suffering of other human beings, and not because they want to make a profit.

But Weiss is evidently right to draw our attention to the strong market dynamic that functions as part of the multibillion-dollar humanitarian sector. It does indeed make sense to talk of supply and demand, competition, market distortions, monopolies, cost, price, efficiencies, and investor bias. These are hard facts in the way the money flows in emergencies, and aid operators rise to meet them. The market is not the whole truth about the global humanitarian project, but it is an important element of the truth.

Weiss also asks us to think metaphorically about the humanitarian profession as a business. In doing so, some of the humanitarian market's irrationality and imperfections, which we tend to indulge as part of our tradition, fast appear as glaring folly. I will just mention two of Weiss's many examples because they are the ones he is most passionate about. The first centers on the efficiency of delivery, and the second on the extraordinary market distortions created by political interests.

Weiss has been a long-time prophet calling for greater organizational efficiency and effectiveness in the UN system. Here, he extends his call to the sector of nongovernmental organizations (NGOs) as well. True to form, Weiss is not cowed by any requirements of diplomatic niceties in his description of most international institutions engaged in humanitarian action. UN agencies are rife with "inertia" and "ineptitude." The Office for the Coordination of Humanitarian Affairs has made "very little difference" and the Good Humanitarian Donorship initiative is "rhetoric only." There is a "glut" of NGOs with no real assurance of quality and a dominant self-interested concern for "turf." When money is in play, all agencies compete amongst each other, and their main concern is organizational survival.

That this critique is hardly new makes it the more frustrating, as Weiss points out. His solution to the problem of the aid operators is very business-like: the sector should be rationalized by a spate of mergers that enhance specialization and efficiency; UN agencies should be consolidated, as recommended back in 1997 by Maurice Strong; and NGOs should focus on achieving the real impact of collective action that some of the big transnational NGOs are beginning to achieve in their own organizational families.

Political bias is perhaps the main feature of the humanitarian market that Weiss puts under the spotlight in this book. If Western government donors are regarded as the major shareholders in the humanitarian business, then they drive extraordinary distortions in a market rhetorically based on need. Weiss is extremely critical of this obvious "market failure," which shows all too clearly that the current market does not work for the majority of victims of war and disaster. The huge distortions in favor of Afghanistan in recent years show that this is a market skewed toward political profit not humanitarian demand.

Weiss has once again written a frank and well-informed book about how to improve international institutions. His emphasis on rationalizing humanitarian institutions, improving evidence-based planning, and increasing donor and agency accountability is right on the nail. As new powers take up more space at the UN in the years ahead, it will become clear where their interests lie in the world's nascent system of global humanitarian aid. Members like China, India, Brazil, Mexico, Nigeria, and Indonesia may seek greater institutional efficiencies, but they may also seek a re-politicization rather than a de-politicization in the spread of humanitarian funds.

In the meantime, every humanitarian who has a purchase on the system would be wise to raise the value, integrity, and reputation of the humanitarian product by following Weiss's three recommendations to rationalize, prove, and account for what they are doing to help people suffering from war and disaster. In doing this, humanitarian principles will still be the best guide to the quality of the humanitarian business. On this point, Weiss and I probably disagree because he is more pessimistic about the possibilities for impartiality and independence than I am. But, for me, these principles and a determination to reach them remains the real mark of profit in any humanitarian business.

Humanitarian aid is not yet an especially big business. At current annual volumes nearing $18 billion, it is about the same size as the Chinese domestic market for soy sauce and other specialty condiments. As China's economy grows and disasters rise around the world, it will indeed be interesting to see which market – soy sauce or humanitarian aid – expands faster and more efficiently to meet demand.

Hugo Slim, University of Oxford, April 2012

Acknowledgments

One of the pleasant tasks of writing a book is to thank those who have helped along the way. This volume for Polity Press condenses my own and others' thinking about the shape of the contemporary humanitarian delivery system in a user-friendly way that nonetheless raises all of the fraught issues. Let me repeat what I wrote in earlier volumes, namely that I am grateful to Louise Knight, who is a wonderful commissioning editor, using a congenial mix of flattery and tough reviews to extract what I trust is a solid scholarly and commercial product.

I have been laboring in the analytical vineyard of humanitarian action for a quarter of a century. Many of my ideas and insights, such as they are, have been catalyzed and developed in a series of collaborations over the years. I have been extremely fortunate in finding intellectual partners.

Let me acknowledge my intellectual debt to those whose work and influence are evident in these pages because much of what I have written here draws on earlier collaborations with several of them. I will begin with Larry Minear, with whom I actively collaborated for ten years on the Humanitarianism & War Project, which we founded and directed. Lessons-learned versus lessons-spurned was the theme song of our efforts from 1990 to 1998, and I draw on our joint efforts from that time.[1] During that period, I benefited from work with Cindy Collins, at the time a graduate student at Brown University.[2] Also these pages reflect work with another younger comrade-in-arms, Don Hubert, who was an essential part of my team at the Research Directorate for the International Commission on Intervention and State Sovereignty (ICISS) in producing *The Responsibility to Protect* and an accompanying research volume.[3] During ICISS's deliberations and in the years that followed, I learned particularly from the work of three of the commissioners: Gareth Evans, Michael Ignatieff, and Ramesh Thakur.[4] I would also like to acknowledge another younger side-kick, Peter J. Hoffman, who went from my classroom to ICISS to introducing me to the theory of new wars and new humanitarianisms in a co-authored book and several articles, and also has now finished his dissertation on private military and security companies.[5] Finally, Michael Barnett and I collaborated over the last several years, first on an edited book and more recently an authored one that seek to re-examine humanitarian shibboleths and rethink standard operating procedures and principles.[6] I am also grateful to several publishers for permission to adapt material here.

Two respected colleagues with critical eyes provided comments on an earlier draft of the manuscript. I begin by thanking Stephen Hopgood, who brought to bear his own cutting-edge work at the School for Oriental and African Studies on the people, the problems, and the prospects of humanitarian action. Anyone who has not read his *Keepers of the Flame: Understanding Amnesty International*[7] should do so to understand many of the motivations behind the generations of human rights advocates.

I am grateful to Hugo Slim not only for his comments but also for the fact that in his Foreword he has graced this book with some of his unusual insights. He is one of those rare individuals who has successfully combined applied university teaching and practical humanitarian work for more than a quarter-century. I only recently discovered what I should have suspected, namely that Hugo draws on his original training as a theologian. As such, he was one of an important group of British "scholar practitioners" – including Mark Duffield, Alex de Waal, David Keen, and Peter Walker – who were joined by a few of us on the other side of the Atlantic in trying to infuse humanitarian ethics into mainstream practice. His own classic treatment of the morality of civilian protection, *Killing Civilians: Method, Madness and Morality in War*,[8] is a text in military academies as well as in departments of international relations and war studies.

In the process of writing this volume and preparing it for publication, I have encountered one particular debt of gratitude. Danielle Zach is completing her dissertation on diasporas and armed conflict at The City University of New York's Graduate Center, and I expect great things from her in the near future. She also has labored tirelessly as an editor for several publications during her student years at 365 Fifth Avenue. In addition to accomplishing such for this volume, she helped me from the very outset to conceptualize and hone the framework of the marketplace in order to depict the numerous interactions of politics and economics in the contemporary international humanitarian system. It was a pleasure to have had her in my classes and as a collaborator over the last several years. This book is immeasurably better because of her careful attention to details and clarity.

The City University of New York's Graduate Center has been my congenial institutional home since 1998. Public universities everywhere are under attack, and I am proud to say that I am part of a system that still strives to provide both excellence and access. I am thankful to President William Kelly and Provost Chase Robinson for warmly and generously supporting my adventures over the years.

This book is dedicated to my daughters, Hannah and Rebeccah, and my grandchildren, Amara and Kieran. They are constant reminders that what once seemed unimaginable is quite possible.

As always, I welcome comments from readers. And obviously, any howlers are my responsibility.

T.G.W., New York, August 2012

Introduction

"Humanitarian" and "business" are juxtaposed in the title of this book for two reasons: provocation and accuracy. Like the expression "humanitarian politics," this title will be unsettling and perhaps even jarring for those who idealize the humanitarian endeavor. Both are provocative because the adjective has essentially uncontested positive connotations while the nouns usually are associated with wheeling and dealing and thus are at odds with the values and self-image of true-believers. Rooted essentially in morality and principle – the parable of the "Good Samaritan" often comes to mind – humanitarian undertakings are seen as noble. The objective is to help people whose lives are at grave risk, irrespective of who they are, or where they are located, or why they are in need.

If humanitarian action claims the moral high ground, the labels of "politics" and "business" are customarily seen to reside elsewhere, in the nether lands. Politics, as Harold Lasswell so famously put it, is essentially about "who gets what, when, how."[1] In practice, it is the art of the possible and associated not with principles but with the compromise of principles in order to get things done. Politicians operate in an arena where deals are cut, money buys access, the common good is ignored, talk is cheap, and tough decisions deferred. As ideal types, humanitarians are interested in the welfare of those in their care and are ideally unaffected by political factors in the countries that provide or receive relief and within the aid agencies that deliver it. Of course in reality, humanitarians are not divorced from politics but rather are steeped in politics at all levels. The day-to-day functioning of all aid agencies intersects in myriad ways with home and host governments, with armed insurgents as well as peacekeepers and local populations, and with the priorities of funding sources. As agents engaged in resource acquisition and distribution, where they get their resources and how and to whom they deliver aid can have significant political consequences, particularly in such contentious environments as war zones. At the same time, humanitarians regularly confront forces that seek to distort and sometimes obstruct assistance for their own political, economic, and military advantage. For political scientists, it is difficult to believe that anyone anywhere is apolitical – and certainly not humanitarians.

While many analysts have moved beyond simplistic interpretations of humanitarian practice, the ideal type of the Good Samaritan exists in many minds as well as in the aspirations and expectations of many aid workers and donors. As David Rieff reminds us, "in the collective memory of modern humanitarianism, the comforting illusion endures that there was a time when relief NGOs [nongovernmental organizations] were largely free to act as they saw fit, taking into account only the needs of the populations they sought to help, and the limits imposed by their own charters."[2]

And while there may be fewer die-hard traditionalists today clinging to a utopian image of humanitarian action than there were yesterday, agencies certainly strategically project a "pure" image to Western publics. As one analyst explained, the marketing logic is crystal clear: NGOs need contributions from donors who wish to have their heartstrings pulled with a story of one suffering child (indeed, two is often too many for the most effective image) who is caught in the crosshairs of war and can only be saved by their donations. Thereafter the donors want to be assured that their contributions are directly helping to improve lives, which then requires the production of brochures depicting relief workers wearing NGO T-shirts posing beside seemingly happy and well-nourished kids. Unsurprisingly a key lesson NGOs teach relief workers is how to pose with children.[3]

Thus, like entrepreneurs, humanitarian agencies are concerned with image and marketing strategies in an expanding global business that over the past two decades has become increasingly competitive with a glut of suppliers vying for their share of the market. In aggregate terms, there is a tremendous need for relief owing to the global political and economic transformations of the past few decades. And while funding is more abundant than ever, resources are still "scarce" given the magnitude of the requirements confronting those who provide succor. For die-hard humanitarians who claim to be apolitical and are often appalled by the allegation that they are not, the very use of the term "business," or "market," will conjure up comparable complexities. These true-believers undoubtedly will be additionally offended by being analyzed as part of a "marketplace." Marketing involves the four "P's" of product, price, place, and promotion. While humanitarians focus on delivery of the product, they should also be increasingly aware of the crucial importance of the entire humanitarian business, which, as Hugo Slim reminds us, begins with "selling the idea of restraint and compassion in war."[4]

Yet this is the reality of humanitarianism in the twenty-first century in a globalizing world. An apt illustration is captured in a photo on a postcard from Médecins sans Frontières (MSF, translated as Doctors without Borders) advertising a talk titled "At Any Price?" It depicts an MSF worker, clad in a T-shirt with the organization's logo, intensely negotiating access to vulnerable populations with child soldiers dressed in military uniform and carrying machine guns. As marketization

encroaches on the traditional humanitarian sector, everything may have a price – from access, to moral authority, and
perhaps even lives.

The Humanitarian Marketplace in the Twenty-first Century

This book is fundamentally about the political economy of
humanitarian assistance and protection as well as the incentives that help explain action and inaction, success and failure.
The contemporary humanitarian marketplace is shaped by
the complexly intertwined disintegrative and integrative
forces of globalization – what James Rosenau once dubbed
"fragmegration."[5] On the one hand, the world is increasingly interconnected through global markets and technology.
Neoliberalization, with its trappings of privatization, liberalization, and deregulation, has fostered economic integration,
eroding barriers to trade in formerly protected markets.
Technological advances ease economic transactions and make
possible the instantaneous flow of information from one side
of the globe to another. At the same time, the development
of universal human rights as well as an increasingly accepted
international responsibility to protect victimized populations regardless of borders has generated a robust normative
framework for the world's affairs.

On the other hand, some integrative trends can have destabilizing effects in fragile states. "Developmentally challenged"
countries are especially vulnerable to external pressures, from
global markets as well as powerful world actors, including
other states and international financial institutions. They are
also more prone to internal upheaval, which at the extreme
means a violent challenge to the state's authority.

Today's civil wars are often intimately linked into global
trade networks in illicit arms, natural resources, and drugs;

and thus tend to be protracted as "mutually hurting stale-mates" fail to materialize with a steady stream of resources. At the same time, they typically produce massive suffering among civilian populations, who frequently are the very targets of violence by belligerents. The immediate drivers of today's marketplace are countries in which governments fail to provide collective goods for their citizens, especially protection from mass murder, forced displacement, and rape – that is, in places where the state abuses its own population or is contested, weak, or even nonexistent, as Afghanistan and Somalia aptly illustrate. Such environments not only generate an enormous demand for lifesaving aid but are also fertile ground for those who seek to profit from misery; and thus they prolong it by distorting the distribution of relief for their own ends.

Alongside high demand for help from suffering civilians, the development of international human rights norms has added incentives for states and the private sector alike to do something and disincentives for doing nothing, which undoubtedly has also contributed to the expansion of the humanitarian sector in terms of both actors and resources. Acts of "shaming" especially are facilitated by global media, which sometime come close to producing "disaster pornography" for headlines.

In a neoliberal global context, it is unsurprising that the "spirit of capitalism" is reshaping humanitarianism. The picture is far more complicated than in abstract economic models that are divorced from political realities and take the existence of a stable state as a given. Indeed alongside neoliberalization, it is the privatization of violence that has fostered the marketization of humanitarian discourses and practices. For-profit businesses have entered the fray of service delivery and protection; belligerent nonstate actors (NSAs) commodify access to victims; aid agencies concern themselves with marketing and branding in a competition for scarce resources from governments as well as corporations.

The "pay-offs" for "suppliers" and "buyers" in the global humanitarian market are varied – the actual alleviation of human suffering is but one among others. Among the "buyers" of humanitarian services are governments, intergovernmental organizations (IGOs), corporations, and individuals (i.e., compositely "donors"). Contributing to saving lives can be a means to another end, a by-product in the pursuit of less lofty goals, including re-election, security, "soft power," a positive corporate image, and even raw financial profit. To be fair, while for-profit firms may be an alternative supplier for relief, they may also help aid agencies do their jobs better if appropriate solidarity or incentives prevail. "Private sector companies," observes António Guterres, current head of the Office of the UN High Commissioner for Refugees (UNHCR), "are also increasingly willing to share their resources and know-how with UNHCR and its humanitarian partners."[6] Typical "suppliers" would obviously include aid agencies, but also for-profit actors such as private military and security companies (PMSCs). Governments can also be direct suppliers of goods and services, while aid agencies themselves can be buyers, for example by contracting PMSCs or local NGOs, or even by purchasing access to needy populations from warlords who are responsible for generating the "demand" in the first place.

This book aims to unpack the dynamics of competition and exchange within the supply chain – which itself constitutes a complex supply and demand network – and the consequences for local economies and those who are the ultimate consumers of humanitarian aid: war victims. As the relationship between suppliers and the consumers of humanitarian aid is essentially a redistributive one, there typically is no direct instrumental exchange between them. Of course, there have been egregious cases of exploitation, in which providers have commodified the very war victims whom they are supposed to help: for example, by requiring girls to perform sexual "labor" in exchange for access to goods and services or cash.

Acting in a particular war zone clearly has dramatic consequences for the profile and financial health of aid agencies. The 2011 global bottom line is some $18 billion and would strike most MBAs, on the face of it, as a substantial commercial opportunity. Some individual agencies (like the International Rescue Committee, IRC) or federations (like Oxfam and Save the Children) are big businesses, while others are far smaller, some even artisanal enterprises. Values purportedly distinguish humanitarians, in big and small enterprises, from their for-profit business counterparts. However, the emerging issue of corporate social responsibility as an issue for corporate boards and stockholders suggests that values also may make for good business. A host of other considerations arise for both humanitarians and business-people, ranging from corruption to transparency. Moreover, if providing goods and services and protecting the vulnerable are the ultimate goals, what if for-profit businesses can provide more bang for the buck or euro and save more lives than private voluntary agencies? What exactly is the value-added of not-for-profit humanitarian organizations? The market drives business, but it also drives humanitarians. And neither is a fan of regulation but rather each looks to the famous or infamous invisible hand. Naomi Klein has even gone so far as to describe the business model behind providing emergency relief as "disaster capitalism."[7]

In short, "humanitarian business" is a very useful and appropriate lens through which to analyze the dynamics of supply and demand and thus understand the challenges of coming to the rescue in the twenty-first century. The last two decades have severely tested the tensile strength of the global safety net. Desperate people still require relief and protection from abuse of their fundamental human rights, yet the political and military conditions that generate the demand for humanitarian action have changed, and so it should not surprise us that so too has the nature of the suppliers in the marketplace.

Along with politics, the metaphor of the marketplace and business economics appears throughout the text. While aid agencies are committed to saving lives and not making profits, nonetheless they respond to incentives and the nature of local and international market forces in order to thrive and "stay in business." Other actors relevant for contemporary humanitarianism actually seek profits. Indeed, PMSCs have become ubiquitous in such war zones as Afghanistan, Iraq, Somalia, and Sudan. Meanwhile, governments are looking for a pay-off from policies and decisions – a reasonable return on the time and resources invested – such as furthering geostrategic interest and domestic political capital. In a world without unlimited resources, it is necessary to determine the opportunity costs for humanitarian decisions.

Moreover, aid is not distributed in a vacuum. Countries riddled with violence and weak rule of law are fertile ground to profit from misery, whether by hoarding aid to drive up food prices, black marketing essential goods, or employing "shadow" workers to pad the payroll. They are high-risk environments with high-risk stakes in which various types of market distortions (such as nepotism, fraud, and corruption) play dominant roles.

Glimpses into the chaotic world of humanitarian action in these dangerous environments regularly appear on television and in the press. The images are poignant: forcibly displaced people on the move and shuffling along dusty roads or wandering around in tent villages surrounded by barbed wire; men and boys (and some women and girls) brandishing automatic weapons amidst destroyed urban and rural landscapes; and sacks of food stamped with UN or NGO acronyms or symbols. The casual viewer or reader might recall a handful of dramatic cases – recently in Libya, Syria, Darfur, Afghanistan, and the Democratic Republic of the Congo (DRC), and earlier in East Timor, Kosovo, Iraq, Haiti, and Somalia. But only a specialist would be aware of another fifty wars raging at present largely beyond the scrutiny of the media. These "silent" or "forgotten" or "orphan" armed conflicts as well as the louder and more visible ones have taken countless lives over the last two decades. Because of warfare, some 35 million of our global neighbors will be homeless tonight as refugees or internally displaced persons (IDPs); they of course join those more numerous homeless who are victims of chronic poverty. In early 2012, an estimated 50 million people were under duress in humanitarian emergencies in 16 countries. Every day aid workers risk their lives to reach the needy, especially in conflict contexts where roads are often impassible and under attack, where food and fuel and medicine are stolen by combatants. This is the so-called real world of humanitarian action in war zones where the risks are high and so is the demand for assistance and protection.

Some Definitions

The terrain that we are about to enter is fraught with ambiguous language and contested concepts. The definitions of key concepts would be helpful as a baseline for readers to interpret what follows. The first is *humanitarian action*. The meaning is relatively straightforward: the delivery of life-saving succor and the protection of the fundamental human rights of endangered populations. Both of these tasks are meant to catch in the global safety net those who are vulnerable because they are being whipped about in the vortex of human-made disasters.

As becomes clearer, the two tasks are mutually reinforcing, although many humanitarians have sought to specialize and insulate one from the other lest by making the provision of life-saving succor subservient to rights, emergency relief be held hostage to human rights advocacy.

And so, what precisely is *humanitarianism*, and who exactly qualifies as a *humanitarian?* For many audiences, "humanitarian" retains great resonance, but one searches in vain for an unequivocal definition, in international law and elsewhere. The International Court of Justice (ICJ) was provided an opportunity in the *Nicaragua v United States* case, when it was asked to clarify what actions legitimately fall within the category of humanitarian behavior. But in its 1986 decision that ruled in favor of Nicaragua and against the United States (which had laid mines in Nicaraguan territorial waters), the ICJ waffled. Instead, it pointed to the principles held by one humanitarian actor and engaged in begging the legal question by stating that humanitarian action is what the International Committee of the Red Cross (ICRC) does.

The dictionary is not much more helpful. The *Oxford English Dictionary* – whose 1819 edition had the first citation – relied on derivatives and tautologies when stating that humanitarian is "having regard to the interests of humanity or mankind at large; relating to, or advocating, or practising humanity or human action."[8] In common discourse, humanitarianism (noun) consists of actions to improve human well-being or welfare, a humanitarian (noun) is a person who actively promotes human welfare, and humanitarian (adj.) usually means philanthropic or charitable.

The ICJ's "definition" requires that we briefly spell out the gold standard espoused by the ICRC, which may make clearer why terms like "politics" and "business" can be so appalling to humanitarians. The standard entails: the independent, neutral, and impartial provision of relief to victims of armed conflicts and natural disasters – in short, to save those at immediate risk of death. The politics of helping when a natural disaster strikes are often relatively simple and thus do not really concern us here. Political authorities who are unable to respond adequately or are temporarily overwhelmed by an unexpected crisis usually welcome with open arms external assistance from whatever the source, be they governments (including their military forces), IGOs, or NGOs. Every country, no matter how sophisticated and developed, can encounter a disaster resembling the 2011 tsunami and Fukushima nuclear meltdown; and in such circumstances, it would be unusual not to seek outside help. In cases of natural disaster, the provision of life-saving resources to populations in need does not usually have an impact on the political status quo in the recipient country. Rather, the political impact of not responding adequately might very well mark the end of the government. The potential cost of not asking for outside assistance thus outweighs the costs of going it alone.

Helping in the midst of violence and especially in civil wars is another matter, however, considerably more fraught and controversial. Governments in the throes of armed conflict, whether domestic or international, often view the acceptance of help as an all-too-visible sign of weakness. Conversely, political officials may look upon aid and protection as fungible resources that are part of the calculations of winning a war. Belligerents are not averse to employing assistance and civilians as weapons. Intrastate armed conflicts (or civil wars) are more freewheeling than international wars waged between professional armies with defined battle lines and rules. The mediation skills of village elders and politicians are outmatched by drugged-up children wielding AK-47s.

The ICRC's ground rules focus not only on what humanitarianism is supposed to do, but also how it is supposed to do it. In his famous desiderata, Jean Pictet, the organization's vice president, identified seven defining principles: humanity, impartiality, neutrality, independence, voluntary service, unity, and universality. The first four arguably constitute the core.[9] Humanity commands attention to all people. Impartiality requires that assistance be based on need and not discriminate on the basis of nationality, race, religion, gender, or political affiliation. Neutrality demands that humanitarian organizations refrain from taking part in hostilities or from any action that either benefits or disadvantages the parties to an armed conflict. Independence necessitates that assistance not be connected to any of the belligerents or others (especially states) with a stake in the outcome of a war; accordingly, there is a general rule that agencies should either refuse or limit their reliance on government funding, especially from those with interests in the outcome.

The ICRC derived these principles from decades of experience regarding which principles best helped to do its job. In other words, although many humanitarians treat these principles as a sacred part of their identity, they have also instrumentally served essential functions. Simply put, traditional principles have helped guide humanitarians to reach people in duress. If aid agencies are perceived by combatants as partial, allied with the opposing side, or having a vested interest in the outcome, they have a difficult time getting access; or, even worse, they may become targets. If principles are followed and respected, both aid workers and victims have a sanctuary of sorts. Operating according to these principles and being perceived as apolitical are particularly important during times of armed conflict. In sum, humanitarianism is defined as the desire and ability to provide life-saving assistance while honoring the principles of humanity, neutrality, impartiality, and independence.

Many observers find that *humanitarian space* is a useful way to conceptualize the physical arena in which humanitarians act. What is this sanctuary? It is ideally a safe area administered and occupied by international aid agencies in a region in which war is taking place. In short, it is a physically secure environment in which victims can be assisted by humanitarians. The image has the advantage of implying that space can open and close, expand and contract. Like everything in this business, it has been subjected to a variety of interpretations, customarily tailored to fit the needs of particular situations or of humanitarian agencies to emphasize aspects of action. The main understandings include: physical access by agencies; the ability within such space of agencies to adhere to traditional principles; and the ability of affected populations to have assistance and protection. So, it is important to specify whether the person or entity referring to "space" wishes to capture the objectives of aid agencies, their ability to respond, the context in which action takes place, or the ability of vulnerable populations to survive.[10]

Finally, what is *humanitarian intervention?* Adam Roberts is clear: "coercive action by one or more states involving the use of armed force in another state without the consent of its authorities, and with the purpose of preventing widespread suffering or death among the inhabitants."[11] Military interventions beginning in the 1990s – against the wishes of a government, or without their genuine consent, and with substantial humanitarian justifications – figure prominently in many of the illustrations throughout this book. The contested nature of the undertaking itself and of the immediate and longer-term results has led two authors recently to ask, "Can intervention work?"[12] While their answer and mine is "yes," we should qualify that by stating that it can do so when it takes place under the proper conditions and with understanding of the local culture and of humanitarian limitations. That, of course, is a tall order.

Here we should spend another moment understanding the notion more broadly. The general meaning of "intervention" can be gleaned from the contexts in which it occurs and the purposes for which it is invoked. Intervention is not involved when an action is based on a genuine and freely given request from, or with the unqualified consent of, a state. Other forms of interference that fall short of coercion in the domestic affairs of a state thus do not amount to intervention. The simplicity of the notion can be muddled somewhat in that foreign policy in general aims to persuade or sometimes cajole other states to change behavior. The absolute absence of consent is required to merit the label of "intervention" because otherwise any outside involvement or attempt to influence or interfere with another political authority would qualify. If it covers everything, the term loses salience.

In a world of asymmetrical power, what constitutes "consent" may also be of questionable relevance. Some observers believe that economic leverage and foreign direct investment may be considered as "intervention," a position that falls on sympathetic ears in an era of contested globalization when smaller countries experience new vulnerabilities about which they can do virtually nothing. A cash-starved developing country can hardly turn down a "request" from the International Monetary Fund (IMF). Some "requests" for military assistance (e.g., by the government of Indonesia in East Timor in 1999) may take place after so much arm-twisting that they actually verge on coercion – a term, "coercive inducement," was coined to reflect this possibility.[13] Nonetheless, consent has a distinct international legal character; and its actual expression is a crucial conceptual distinction for military measures against a state as well as for such non-military measures as political and economic sanctions, arms embargoes, and international criminal prosecution.[14]

About the Book

Chapter 1, "Responding to Humanitarian Demands," begins with antecedents in the anti-slavery movement, the response to social ills wrought by the expansion of industrial capitalism, and efforts to curb colonial rapaciousness. It then moves to discuss the three historical periods of consequence for this book: the late nineteenth-century founding of the International Committee of the Red Cross to World War II; the Cold War humanitarian system, 1945–89; and the present period beginning after the end of the Cold War. The following section provides an overview of the diverse actors that flock to any human-made disaster from outside a war zone: NGOs; the ICRC; bilateral aid agencies; members of the UN system; the military; for-profit actors (corporations and PMSCs); and the media. There will also be a discussion of local actors, including those responsible for generating demand – that is, armed belligerents who can obstruct as well as facilitate the distribution of aid – as well as NGOs and businesses that can be an essential part of the supply chain.

Chapter 2 focuses on our turbulent times and is titled "The Contemporary Landscape: Need and Greed." It explores the playing field of contemporary humanitarians: new wars and new humanitarianisms. The main focus is the security threats that transnationalized domestic armed conflicts pose to civilians, communities, and even entire regions. Part of the international response by governments to such destabilization has been to increase overall funding for humanitarian services, including through their own bilateral aid programs. At the same time, the dangerous context in which humanitarian actors typically operate – indeed they are ever more frequently the very targets of kidnapping and violence – has also led to the commodification of protection and access. Paying for such goods and services often fosters uncomfortable decisions and sometimes ethical dilemmas. War-torn countries are high-risk environments with high-risk stakes.

Chapter 3, "Coordination vs. Competition in an Unregulated Market," explores the history of largely unsuccessful efforts to pull together the various moving parts of the international humanitarian system. An essential component of the analysis consists of the UN's efforts – successively the UN Disaster Relief Organization (UNDRO), the Department of Humanitarian Affairs (DHA), and the Office for the Coordination of Humanitarian Affairs (OCHA) – and various NGO efforts – including the formation of federations such as Save the Children and Oxfam as well as the coalitions Inter-Action and Voluntary Organizations in Cooperation in Emergencies (VOICE) in the US and Europe, respectively. Numerous experiments to attenuate atomization contain lessons. The chapter concludes with an analysis of how competition for resources and turf among agencies can undermine the collective endeavor of saving lives and foster niche specialization (e.g., health, shelter, food), which may improve delivery within specific sectors.

Chapter 4 examines "Market Distortions from Above and Below." It confronts head-on some of the most acute problems within the humanitarian sector itself. Aid organizations operate within contexts that present ethical dilemmas and complications resulting from waste, inefficiency, and corruption. In addition, the kinds of topics that enter an introductory economics course come to the fore, namely the size of the market and competition as well as concerns with what are often called "black" (or parallel) markets in which "taxation" from belligerents is seen as the cost of doing business. Other opportunities for rent-seeking and the negative externalities resulting from aid economies are also discussed.

Chapter 5 is titled "The Push and Pull of Coming to the

Rescue." While they make frequent appearances earlier, this is the occasion to unpack in some detail two related topics. The first is the impact of September 11, 2001, and the war on terror on the nature of humanitarian action. The second is the responsibility to protect (R2P), the most significant normative development of our times, which is situated at the coalface of world politics and international relations: state sovereignty. Both developments will help to shed light on the unevenness in responses, by governments and humanitarians, to crises and will necessarily draw in the issues of choosing high-profile emergencies over less publicized ones.

Chapter 6 permits me to ask and hazard a few answers to "What Next?" This concluding chapter does not suggest structural reforms that could decrease the demand for humanitarian action by tackling the root causes of conflict. That is far beyond this author's feeble imagination. Hence, it leaves complex debates within international political economy about such pertinent issues as global wealth redistribution, trade policy, and technology transfer to more capable specialists in that field. What appears instead are some thoughts about pragmatic reform that could and should be considered by the humanitarian sector itself.

In particular, I revisit three ideas that have preoccupied me for some time. The first is the urgent need for the seemingly impossible task of consolidation or centralization of the international humanitarian system. The second consists of mechanisms to increase accountability and transparency. The third is the requirement for a more thoughtful humanitarianism, of more basic research as part of an effort to pursue a humanitarian science (i.e., something akin to military science).

It is now time to enter the humanitarian marketplace.

CHAPTER ONE

Responding to Humanitarian Demands

This chapter provides an overview of the actors that flock to any human-made disaster from outside the war zone in question. International "suppliers" consist of an unlikely group of bedfellows: NGOs; the ICRC; members of the UN system; bilateral aid agencies; the military; and for-profit actors (corporations and private military companies). Within specific war zones, they interact not only with one other but also with local actors, such as belligerents, who control access to humanitarian space, and representatives of civil society organizations and businesses, who participate in the delivery assistance "supply chain."

This chapter begins with a brief history of the humanitarian idea and three distinctive historical periods: the founding of the International Committee of the Red Cross to World War II; the Cold War humanitarian system, 1945–89; and the turbulent present. The basic distinction between the politics of helping in natural disasters and in wars also figures in the discussion.

A Brief History of Humanitarianism

Michael Barnett's masterful treatment of the history of humanitarianism argues that its origins are found in transformations in the late eighteenth century, specifically the first rumblings of the abolitionist movement.[1] The issue for these idealists was not to save lives at immediate risk because of warfare but rather to alleviate the suffering caused by another human-made tragedy, slavery. The movement's success was facilitated by the economic impediments that slavery imposed on the expansion of industrial capitalism, which meant that those with moral concerns were on the same side of the barricades as capitalists.

The most relevant contemporary forms of humanitarianism, as Craig Calhoun argues, began in the nineteenth century as a consequence primarily of the coming together of the forces of production and salvation.[2] The context was the perceived breakdown of society and emergence of moral ills that were being caused by rapid industrialization, urbanization, and market expansion. Karl Polanyi's seminal work articulates the perverse effects of capitalism on traditional social order, which intimately tied economic organization to social relationships through systems of redistribution and reciprocity. With the rise of industrial capitalism, he argued, production was extracted from society, which became subordinated to the needs of the "self-regulating" market. The result was massive social dislocation and efforts to protect society from the vagaries of *laissez-faire* capitalism.[3]

Drawing from a mixture of religious and Enlightenment ideas, various intellectuals, politicians, jurists, and clergy adopted the language of humanitarianism to describe their proposed social and political reforms and to push for public action to alleviate suffering. The result was the formation of social movements to foster temperance, charity for the poor, regulations regarding child labor, and mass education. Marxists critiqued such efforts as mere "bourgeois reform" because by providing a palliative to the ills produced by capitalism, humanitarian and philanthropic initiatives sustained an inherently exploitative system. In the short term they eased suffering, but in the long term they thwarted meaningful societal change.

In addition to counter-movements to slavery and free-market capitalism, modern humanitarianism's roots can be traced to efforts to mitigate colonial exploitation. The relationship between colonialism and humanitarianism is more complicated than the reductionist view that the latter was merely an outgrowth of and justification for imperialism.[4] The basis for that simplistic view relies on an easy target, the unsavory King Leopold's rapacious exploitation of the Belgian Congo as advancing civilization and as a "humanitarian" project.[5] Missionaries frequently could be "civilizing" agents, easing the way for external domination. Yet there were instances in which missionaries called for reform and action that were at odds with imperial interests; some were outraged by the un-Christian behavior of colonial governments and foreign merchants who engaged in all forms of debauchery and exploitation.[6] And in the late nineteenth century, various organizations began to express doubts about conversions on the grounds that they denigrated local traditions, customs, and cultures. Thus, although humanitarianism was often invoked as an alibi for interest-based imperial interventions, it sometimes stood in stark opposition to colonial sentiments as well.

If we are to pinpoint the inaugural moment for war-related international humanitarianism, it was in 1864 with the establishment of the International Committee of the Red Cross and the emergence of international humanitarian law.[7] During the 1859 Battle of Solferino, the Swiss businessman Henry Dunant witnessed wounded soldiers callously abandoned on the battlefield to die, which prompted him to propose the creation of relief societies with trained volunteers to assist injured combatants in times of war. We begin our treatment of humanitarian action in war zones here. The popularity and resonance of Dunant's idea were surprising: within three years the grassroots campaign produced the ICRC and the

Geneva Conventions. Dunant was awarded the first Nobel Peace Prize in 1901, and the ICRC has stood as the industry standard since. A failed effort in Brussels in 1874 to consider a draft of the laws of war drawn up by Russian Tsar Alexander II met with more success in 1899 and 1907, when it became the basis of the Hague Conventions.

Humanitarianism's next great leap forward – ironically but predictably – was as a consequence of the two world wars of the twentieth century. In terms of institution-building, many familiar contemporary NGOs and IGOs emerged in reaction to the forces of destruction unleashed by those world-wide cataclysms. In response to the refugees caused by the Russian Revolution, the League of Nations established the High Commission for Russian Refugees (1920–2), headed by Fridtjof Nansen, who subsequently expanded his mandate to include other continental populations. Two holdovers from his efforts, the Intergovernmental Committee for Refugees and the High Commissioner for Refugees, fused in 1943 to form the UN Relief and Rehabilitation Administration (UNRRA). NGOs, in most cases, were running ahead of states in the area of refugee relief: for example, Russian refugees prompted two sisters, Eglantyne Jebb and Dorothy Buxton, to found Save the Children in 1919, while the birth of the Nazi regime led the famous refugee Albert Einstein to found an American branch of the European-based International Relief Association in 1933, which later merged with the Emergency Rescue Committee in 1942 to form the International Rescue Committee.

Except for the ICRC and a handful of NGOs, however, few organizations thought of themselves as permanent. Instead, most came and went in order to respond to an emergency. However, after World War II a new generation of agencies arose to assist European victims; they subsequently developed a global reach, and many are still with us. Their permanence introduced a new set of dynamics, including not only the economics of a growing industry and bureaucracies, but also a growing consideration of the purpose of humanitarianism, its proper relationship to states, and the principles guiding actions.

The specter of rampant inhumanity throughout World War II led to hope for a different future – ironically, not the triumph of humanitarianism but rather a response to the utter desecration of the very idea of humanity. The Holocaust, massive displacements, fire bombings, and ultimately the use of nuclear weapons led diplomats and activists to call for the protection of civilians. The search for human dignity led to the construction of such normative humanitarian pillars as the 1945 UN Charter, the 1948 Universal Declaration of Human Rights, the 1948 Convention on the Prevention and Punishment of the Crime of Genocide, and the 1949 Geneva Conventions (and eventually the 1977 Additional Protocols). There also was a growth in intergovernmental and nongovernmental machinery. UNRRA was revamped in 1946 as the International Rescue Organization, which became the UNHCR in 1951; although it was supposed to be a temporary agency limited to European refugees, it soon became a permanent feature in global affairs. The UN Children's Fund, or UNICEF as it is more commonly known, had a similar institutional biography and is now one of the most well known of humanitarian agencies. In 1942 a group of Quakers founded the Oxford Committee for Famine Relief (later shortened to Oxfam) to respond to the appalling famine in Greece during which perhaps half of the children died. Shortly after the end of World War II, Lutheran World Relief, Church World Service, and Caritas International came into being – founded by Lutherans, the US National Council of Churches, and the Vatican, respectively. As mentioned, many of the relief organizations established in response to the needs of

European victims turned their attention to reconstruction and then development following the return or resettlement of the wounded and displaced. Oxfam, the Cooperative for Assistance and Relief Everywhere (better known by its acronym, CARE), and Catholic Relief Services all got their start providing relief during World War II and then turned their attention to poverty alleviation and development.

The tectonic political shifts with the thawing and ultimate end of the Cold War opened the latest chapter in the history of the international humanitarian system. One of its key distinguishing characteristics is the dramatic expansion of "suppliers" in terms of numbers and diversity of organizational approaches. To begin, the sheer growth in NGO numbers alone is nothing short of remarkable.[8] Setting aside for the moment what is and what is not a truly humanitarian organization, there are at least 2,500 international NGOs in the business, although probably only a tenth of them are truly significant.[9] In a no-holds-barred exposé, one journalist cites UN Development Programme (UNDP) estimates that there could be 37,000 international NGOs with some relevance for "the crisis caravan," and that on average 1,000 international and local NGOs show up for any contemporary emergency.[10] Part of what two authors depict as a "swarm"[11] of agencies appearing for a new crisis can be explained by the proliferation of mom-and-pop aid deliverers, sometimes called MONGOs ("my own NGO").

Global longitudinal data are unavailable, but a detailed survey of US-based private voluntary agencies engaged in relief and development is undoubtedly indicative of more general patterns in today's marketplace. Considerable growth has taken place over the last three-quarters of a century. In 1940, shortly after the start of World War II, the number of US-based organizations rose to 387 (from 240), but the numbers dropped to 103 in 1946 and 60 in 1948. They rose steadily thereafter and reached 543 in 2005. The growth was especially dramatic from 1986 to 1994, when the number increased from 178 to 506.[12]

What about the number of aid workers worldwide? Abby Stoddard and her colleagues hazard a guess of over 200,000.[13] But Peter Walker and Catherine Russ are undoubtedly closer to the mark when they confess: "We have no idea what size this population is." Estimates include everyone from cleaning personnel and drivers in field offices to CEOs in headquarters. As a result of vague and inconsistent definitions and poor reporting, Walker and Russ prefer to extrapolate from reliable Oxfam data and estimate that there probably are some 30,000 humanitarian professionals (both local and expatriate) worldwide.[14]

In addition to the growth in numbers of NGOs, other types of actors have become increasingly involved in the delivery of assistance, as we see below. Among these are military forces as well as for-profit firms that typically specialize in security, transportation, and logistics.

What explains the explosion of the sector in the post-Cold War era? Two intertwined global phenomena are key: the collapse of the bipolar system; and the debt crisis of the 1980s, the so-called lost decade, and its international response – neoliberalism. Combined, these factors had a particularly debilitating effect on developing countries, in terms of the state's capacity to deliver public services and maintain a monopoly of violence within its territorial borders.

The neoliberal agenda of the IMF and the World Bank had devastating effects on the most economically vulnerable populations, as the state was trimmed down, public budgets for social services were slashed, and once protected domestic markets were liberalized. Humanitarian agencies and other private organizations closed some of the gaps in the social safety net. For regimes that relied on patronage to sustain their rule, such reforms would fuel instability both from above and from below.

The loss of geostrategic significance of parts of the Third World and the resulting decrease in military and economic aid also added fuel to the fire. The superpower patronage that for decades had propped up illegitimate governments was no longer available to them. The result of these political and economic trends was an increase in civil wars – initially in both absolute terms and relative to international armed conflicts. These would be dubbed "new wars," owing to the combination of characteristics, including mass civilian suffering.

The next chapter addresses whether the dynamics of today's warfare actually are all that new, but humanitarian emergencies certainly were increasingly prominent on the international agenda and in the media spotlight.[15] As states paid more attention, "complex humanitarian emergencies" was an expression coined to depict the ugly and confusing reality of a "conflict-related humanitarian disaster involving a high degree of breakdown and social dislocation and, reflecting this condition, requiring a system-wide aid response from the international community."[16] Gossips observing the UN committee that drafted the definition put forward the view that it reflected the reality that no one really knew what was going on or what to do.

Much like the response to World War II, the growing number of crises that erupted in the turbulent 1990s helped catalyze new movements that were intent on rescuing and protecting civilians at risk. Several features stand out. Perhaps the most prominent was the growing internationalization and institutionalization of human rights, with the United Nations playing the signature role. In particular, the Security Council became more deeply involved in interpreting, protecting, promoting, and monitoring human rights as essential components of peace operations, a development made possible with the end of the East–West rivalry. A most distinctive feature of this period was the council's expansion of what it deemed as constituting a "threat to international peace and security," the trigger for UN involvement. During the Cold War, the council had limited its definition of such threats to disputes between states that might or had become militarized, conflicts involving the great powers, and general menaces to global stability.[17]

One reason why the Security Council redefined peace and security was the emerging relative significance of the so-called new wars. In reaction to the growing perception that domestic armed conflicts were leaving hundreds of thousands of civilians at risk, creating mass flight, and destabilizing entire regions, the council authorized coercive measures on the grounds that war-induced disasters and mass atrocities imperiled regional and international security. Thus, grave humanitarian crises and human rights abuses became part of an expanded definition of what states legitimately viewed as threats to international peace and security.[18]

Perhaps the surest and most controversial expression of the Security Council's new-found interest in human rights and welfare was its willingness to use military force for human protection purposes, or "humanitarian intervention."[19] The Cold War Security Council occasionally acknowledged the existence of humanitarian issues, but faint rhetoric outstripped any willingness to act. No resolution mentioned the humanitarian dimensions of any armed conflict from 1945 until the Arab–Israeli war of 1967, and the first mention of the ICRC was not until 1978.[20] In the 1970s and 1980s "the Security Council gave humanitarian aspects of armed conflict limited priority . . . but the early nineteen-nineties can be seen as a watershed."[21] Resolution 792 in December 1992 broke all records in making 18 references to the "H" word in authorizing US-led action in Somalia. There was no turning back.

The growing involvement of the Security Council in the internal affairs of states and justification of that involvement on humanitarian grounds signaled a none-too-subtle shift in the meaning of sovereignty. States were now expected to respect their citizens or face sanctions. Whereas once their legitimacy had divine origins, now it was dependent on the rule of law, markets, and democratic principles. Essentially state sovereignty was conditional and based on implied contracts between the state and its society and among states. What happened when states either did not satisfy those conditions or broke the contract?

Although there had earlier been whispers of an international duty to protect civilians, most famously in the Convention on the Prevention and Punishment of the Crime of Genocide and in some human rights treaties and norms, the real momentum to actually protect populations from egregious infringements on their rights was a post-Cold War phenomenon. Various statements, documents, events, and forces opened up the normative space for humanitarian intervention. The Security Council legitimated its coercive actions in places such as Somalia because of the need to protect those human beings at risk as a result of civil war. As a consequence of interventions taken (Kosovo and East Timor) and not taken (Rwanda), in 1999 Secretary-General Kofi Annan articulated his doctrine of "two sovereignties."[22] The subsequent diplomatic uproar led to the formation of the International Commission on Intervention and State Sovereignty (ICISS),[23] whose final report argued that when states cannot or will not protect their populations, the international "responsibility to protect" kicks in. We return to this crucial topic in Chapter 5.

Controversy continues about the relationship between the expanding peace and security agenda, humanitarianism, and state interests. Arguably a calculation about the relationship between interests and the potential impacts of humanitarian disasters in an increasingly interconnected world drove the underlying concern to respond vigorously. Complex emergencies had regional and sometimes wider international consequences. Because failed states are a threat to themselves and to others, they must be "saved," and the surest antidote to domestic instability is the creation of stable, legitimate states organized around human rights, markets, and democracy.

With changing state interests and international norms, the military thus became an increasingly prominent actor in the humanitarian arena, not only for the delivery of relief goods and services, but also for the provision of protection for civilians. Agencies that were operational in active war zones had to work alongside troops with greater frequency than in the past and in the midst of belligerents that did not respect international humanitarian law, a topic explored in greater depth in the next chapter. Moreover, since the terrorist attacks of 9/11, many countries, especially the United States, have viewed counter-terrorism and humanitarianism as crime-fighting partners – with failed states as sanctuaries and staging platforms for terrorists. Humanitarian organizations, in this view, can become part of wider "hearts and minds" campaigns, attempting to convince local populations of the righteousness of armies invading in the name of stability and freedom.

Another way that today's sector differs from what preceded is the existence of multiple forms of humanitarian practice. Agencies such as CARE, for example, started development programs alongside their traditional emergency relief, thereby distinguishing them from the ICRC and a handful of other purely emergency organizations. At first there was no explicit debate over the meaning of humanitarianism because those agencies that delivered relief plus something else were content to leave the "humanitarian" label for others. Except during times of war when more resources were in play, there was no reason to wage a terminological battle. Different camps rarely had to interact in the field. Moreover, few complained because many development agencies were also moving to create emergency capacities as demand for them grew. With the growing scope of activities involved in contemporary humanitarian interventions, extending to the actual rebuilding of states in such war-torn societies as Kosovo and East Timor, there is a growing task expansion within relief agencies themselves.

We continue today in the period that began with the end of the Cold War. While we should be able to find a better label than "post-Cold War," we have not yet done so. In many respects the tensions and dilemmas from previous periods continue amidst new ones; the contemporary period is embedded in humanitarian history. Challenges that many observers treat as brand new are as old as humanitarianism itself. However, the post-Cold War era exhibits enough distinctive features to warrant being treated as a separate period. The sheer explosion of aid agencies in all manner of relief and reconstruction is one characteristic; and this booming population of humanitarian suppliers taking on more tasks with burgeoning resources has injected an urgency into the kinds of doubts and questions that were only hinted at earlier. We return to these in the next chapter, when the contemporary landscape is painted in detail.

The Suppliers: A Profile

This section of the chapter spells out the nuts and bolts (values, strengths, weaknesses, and magnitude of operations) that characterize the various types of actors on the contemporary international humanitarian stage. Crucial to contemporary business analysis and to humanitarian action is the notion of multi-stakeholder analysis in order to identify all the relevant actors likely to affect or be affected by a proposed action as well as to assess their weight and interests. Such an approach

Figure 1.1   External and internal actors on the ground

permits identifying the potential impact of any humanitarian effort on all actors. The notion behind this type of analysis for humanitarianism is to assess the diverse and often conflicting interests of all stakeholders and to privilege the needs of affected populations.

Among those that exert influence on the ground from outside a war zone are: international NGOs; the ICRC; members of the UN system; bilateral aid agencies; external military forces; for-profit firms; and the media. Diasporas, which are scattered populations outside the state but inside an "imagined community,"[24] can also be crucial in conflict contexts

with transnational dimensions; however, they are not discussed here, as such populations typically play less of a role
on the ground, preferring to engage in activism (especially
sending funds) from afar. Operating alongside, and sometimes in opposition to, external agents in a particular war zone
are local actors, which include NGOs and businesses as well
as armed belligerents that can act as "suppliers" of access to
suffering populations, often at a price. The "commodification" of humanitarian space has made them important actors
in the contemporary marketplace as well. In the face of new
and soaring demands, the "market for aid" demonstrated a
remarkable capacity to expand the suppliers, the number and
range of players.[25]

Figure 1.1 depicts the external and internal actors that may
respond to humanitarian emergencies. It is a clear snapshot
of the humanitarian business.[26] Needless to say, the pristine
presentation of a two-dimensional illustration is considerably
more convoluted in three dimensions in the fog of war and
the fog of humanitarianism on the ground.

International NGOs

Private relief groups, or nongovernmental organizations, are
often envisioned as the quintessential humanitarian actor
and are a crucial source of support for those suffering from
wars. They include such familiar associations as CARE,
Oxfam, Save the Children, World Vision, MSF, and Catholic
Relief Services; lesser-known but important ones like
the International Rescue Committee and Islamic Relief
Worldwide; and largely unknown ones like Mercy Corps
International. The delivery of emergency relief is dominated
by about 15 to 20 major international NGOs or federations of
national NGOs that have annual budgets of at least $100 mil-
lion and often as large as $1 billion and work in at least eight

to ten countries. This group can be considered an oligopoly. The largest expend as much in a given crisis as many UN organizations and governments. Other NGOs make far more modest contributions to a particular geographical area or to a particular sector. Many NGOs have cultivated active and influential constituencies of individual donors, but the largest often receive the bulk of their funds from governments or subcontracts from UN organizations.

Extreme heterogeneity, in terms of the size of their operations and their approach to issues, makes generalizations about NGOs, even the largest, problematic.[27] Across-the-board characterizations are difficult between giants like World Vision and CARE (with annual budgets over $1 billion) and much smaller operations; between those that carry out operations themselves mainly with expatriate staff and those that work mainly through local counterparts within crises; and between those that accept no funds from governments (e.g., Oxfam-America) to underscore their autonomy and those that are essentially entirely financed by public resources (e.g., the Norwegian Refugee Council). Also, critics are increasingly aware of turf wars that can bedevil overall performance when organizational interests trump those of victims.[28] These are topics to which we return.

For the time being, it is fair to say that the hallmark of NGOs is their link to the grass roots and their action orientation. They are reputed to be more non-bureaucratic, flexible, and creative than their governmental or intergovernmental counterparts; and they are certainly less constrained by legal formalities and diplomatic niceties. NGOs have assumed an increasing importance in the last two decades and can no longer be dismissed simply as "do-gooders." They receive resources as part of the privatization of international relations, and they are endeavoring to improve their professionalism. There are national and international professional associations: for example, the Washington-based InterAction is a consortium of some 200 American private agencies.

The ICRC

The International Committee of the Red Cross occupies an unusual position and thus is treated as a separate type of supplier – in a category by itself. Founded in 1864, it is the oldest international humanitarian organization. It is also the largest outside of the UN system. A private organization with a board of governors of prominent Swiss citizens, the ICRC is like NGOs in that it receives both private and public contributions, but governments typically provide 90 percent of its annual budget, which in 2012 was about $1.2 billion to cover some 11,000 staff in 80 countries. Nonetheless, it does not consider itself an IGO. It is an NSA, but it also does not consider itself an NGO because it is the custodian of the Geneva Conventions signed by states. The ICRC is distinct in that it has a specific recognition in international humanitarian law, for which it is designated the custodian. It enjoys, for example, observer status in the UN General Assembly, and its chief delegate in New York meets regularly with the president of the Security Council. The ICRC enjoys a unique mission under international humanitarian law – such as monitoring the treatment of prisoners of war and detainees, and promoting family reunification. In short, it is in a league of its own.[29]

The ICRC's mandate thrusts it into all of the world's major crises. News reports often rely on ICRC sources, quoting "authoritative ICRC estimates." The ICRC staff are among the most intrepid, preceding the staff from other agencies and remaining in the line of fire after the departure of UN personnel, donor-government officials, and sometimes even UN soldiers (in Rwanda in 1994, for instance).

The ICRC, along with the International Federation

(formerly League) of Red Cross and Red Crescent Societies (IFRC) and its national chapters in some 165 countries, constitute the "Red Cross movement."[30] The ICRC has its headquarters in Geneva and is staffed in key international posts largely by Swiss nationals. For specific assignments, it accepts the services of persons from national societies. Its location in a neutral country and its staffing underscore its mandate under the Geneva Conventions of 1949 and the Additional Protocols of 1977 that effectiveness in the humanitarian arena depends on strict neutrality and impartiality.

Unlike most other humanitarian agencies, the ICRC has clear and carefully elaborated principles, and its disciplined staff is committed to abiding by them. Unlike most NGOs and IGOs, which mount a range of activities from relief to reconstruction and development, the ICRC works only in war zones – both international ones like Iraq–Kuwait or civil wars (which the ICRC prefers to label "non-international wars") like Somalia and Rwanda.

The UN System

The UN system is key to the world's response mechanism for humanitarian disasters. The three largest organizations with responsibilities in human-made disasters are the UNHCR UNICEF, and the World Food Programme (WFP). Their combined resources amounted in 2011 to some $11 billion. Also of central importance to many operations are the UNDP and since 1998 OCHA.

In principle, initiatives by UN organizations are more acceptable than those sponsored by a single government or even a few governments. Complicating rapid and robust decision-making by the United Nations, of course, are the same states with differing perspectives and interests. At the outset, we should note that the term "system" is a misnomer when applied to the entities of the United Nations.[31] The secretary-general is not really the chief executive officer of anything except the UN Secretariat in New York. The executive heads of the other agencies are responsible for their own programs; they raise funds that are comparable to those controlled by the secretary-general himself (not yet herself); and they report to autonomous governing boards.

OCHA is a recent acronym, dating from January 1998. The DHA, its predecessor from 1992 to 1997, was established in response to donor dissatisfaction with the inability of the UN system and international NGOs to coordinate their activities after the Persian Gulf War. UNDRO had been established in 1971 to help in natural catastrophes and was subsumed in the DHA. The major functions of OCHA are consolidated appeals and information-sharing, along with humanitarian diplomacy in New York. Part of the "cabinet" of the UN secretary-general, OCHA is not an operational agency.

From its headquarters in Geneva, the UNHCR is guardian of the 1951 Convention Relating to the Status of Refugees and the 1967 Protocol.[32] Its responsibilities include the protection of refugees, their resettlement into a country of first asylum or elsewhere, and their repatriation to their country of origin when possible. Increasingly, the organization has also been charged with "persons in refugee-like situations" but who have not fled across an international border – namely, internally displaced persons and war victims who have not moved at all. The UNHCR contracts other UN agencies and especially NGOs to implement programs. The UNHCR's budget grew dramatically in the 1990s, peaking in 1994–5 at some $1.3 billion, with about $500 million for the former Yugoslavia and $300 million for Rwanda. It has continued growing in the twenty-first century, with a 2012 budget of about $3.6 billion for its 7,700 staff in 126 countries.

UNICEF – officially the UN Children's Fund, and originally

the UN International Children's Fund, but better known by its brand-name acronym – provides material assistance such as food, clothing, and medical supplies in relief operations while keeping its eye turned toward longer-term development for women and children.[33] Established in 1946 to provide immediate relief to child victims of World War II and now headquartered in Manhattan in its own building across First Avenue from the United Nations, UNICEF receives the bulk of its resources from governments; but about 30 percent comes from private fundraising (an unusual practice for an IGO), including the popular sale of holiday cards and gifts. During the Cold War, UNICEF was unlike other organizations of the UN system and often able to deal with insurgent authorities because of its unusual role in helping the most vulnerable victims, women and children. In 2010, UNICEF's income reached $3.7 billion (its regular budget alone amounted to nearly $1 billion), about one quarter of which was devoted to emergency assistance to cover work in some 190 countries.

Even before the end of World War II, a conference on food insecurity held in Hot Springs, Virginia, led to the founding of a UN specialized agency in waiting, the Food and Agriculture Organization (FAO), which would eventually be created in Rome. But the main humanitarian actor operating from that city is the WFP, which was established as a food-surplus-disposal organization following the World Food Conference of 1974.[34] In 2011 the value of contributions to the WFP amounted to about $3.6 billion. The WFP began with a development orientation, but it now devotes about 80 percent of its efforts to emergencies. It coordinates food shipments with other UN agencies and NGOs. In fact, it has become the logistics specialist within the UN system.

Also in New York are the headquarters for the UNDP, which was established as the central source of funding for technical assistance and pre-feasibility projects within the

UN system. With 129 offices around the globe and a presence on the ground in 176 countries, its program expenditures in 2009 approached $5.4 billion.[35] The senior UNDP official in recipient countries (formerly called the "UNDP resident representative" but now the "UN resident coordinator") normally acts as the point-person for all UN activities in a country. When war erupts, this official may remain to coordinate humanitarian aid; but often he or she is replaced by someone with a greater expertise in emergencies and political negotiations, and sometimes given the additional title of emergency relief coordinator (ERC) or the special representative of the secretary-general (SRSG). After violence has settled down, the UNDP's top official returns to replace the secretary-general's personal envoy and to assume overall responsibilities for reconstruction, rehabilitation, and development.

Observers, especially from outside the United Nations, often question whether the world organization should play such a pivotal humanitarian role in civil wars. As a political organization comprised of member states, the UN has problems in relating to disputing parties without appearing to take sides. Once the Security Council, in particular, gets involved and considers non-forcible or forcible sanctions, it complicates the role of UN humanitarians who endeavor to help civilians on all sides. In addition, an intergovernmental organization whose members are states means that it suffers from an inherent bias against NSAs.

Bilateral Aid Agencies

Governments not only make substantial financial contributions to UN agencies and to NGOs but also operate their own bilateral assistance programs. For example, the Washington-based US Agency for International Development (USAID) and the London-based Department for International

Development (DfID) have their own direct humanitarian assistance programs for many wars, just as they have development assistance projects throughout the world. The kinds of relationships and the resources employed by the major powers with recipient countries are different from those government-to-government ones of middle powers like the Norwegian Agency for Development (NORAD) or the Canadian International Development Agency (CIDA).

Historical, diplomatic, economic, and political relationships of a government within a region may also make it more or less welcome as a bilateral partner when emergency strikes. Because of its traditions and resources, the United States usually plays a major role (oftentimes financing a third or even a half of the bills). But Washington's bilateral aid is often more suspect than that emanating from smaller neutral countries like Austria and Switzerland or such Nordic countries as Sweden and Finland. Former colonial powers, especially France and Britain, have historical links that affect their proclivity to intervene in a region as well as their acceptability – in both positive and negative ways.

European governments, in addition to having their own national aid agencies, have contributed since 1992 through the European Community Humanitarian Office (ECHO). Initially, the role of the former European Community and now European Union was relatively small, serving mainly as a channel for contributions to other European organizations by member states. However, ECHO has continually grown, posted its own staff, and asserted an important financial role in complex emergencies (on average, some $1.3 billion annually).

As might be expected, bilateral or collective European assistance is more vulnerable to active politicization than is UN or NGO assistance. With the end of the Cold War era, bilateral resources have been channeled through IGOs and NGOs by government aid agencies. But that trend has not meant the disappearance of political concerns by governments. Donors are not bashful about exercising control over those resources channeled through intergovernmental and nongovernmental agencies. Pushing their own agendas and priorities is possible because of the leverage flowing from the power of the purse. It is rare for multilateral or nongovernmental organizations to say "no" to such "tied" financing because competitors will readily agree.

Outside Military Forces

Prior to the end of the Cold War, foreign military personnel (even those in UN operations) played an ancillary role in delivering relief or protecting human rights. The five permanent and ten rotating members of the Security Council rarely addressed humanitarian concerns; the narrowest interpretations of nonintervention in the domestic affairs of states, especially with regard to outside military forces, had been the rule. In spite of the bullish-sounding provisions in several articles of the UN Charter, the world organization actually possesses no independent military capacity. The soldiers who serve in UN operations remain part of the armed forces of their own countries and are under their command and control.

Beginning with the creation of space in northern Iraq for victimized Kurds in 1991 following Saddam Hussein's invasion of Kuwait and then his expulsion by a UN-approved coalition, outside military forces frequently have been pressed into service and are now an essential component of the humanitarian supply network. In addition to directly delivering aid to suffering populations, the military can provide a service that the civilian actors discussed above cannot – namely, physical protection to affected populations and security relief convoys for aid agencies.

In examining cases of outside military help, it is important to distinguish two distinct roles and sets of benefits. Sometimes they deploy their heavy-lifting and logistics capacity to transport large quantities of relief supplies to remote locations. Sometimes troops provide physical security or change regimes, thereby creating safer spaces in which aid agencies carry out their activities. As we shall see, such a presence can be expensive, provocative, and overwhelming (from a local perspective). If political support is not firm at home, there can also be blow-back – for instance, the "Somalia syndrome," which resulted in the United States after the dishonorable killing and display of dead US Rangers in Mogadishu.

Observers have difficulties in clearly distinguishing between "delivery" and "protection" – the two components of "humanitarian action" – because they are closely linked.[36] Nonetheless, it is easier to quantify the former than the latter, which is why attention is normally paid to the volume and value of goods and personnel devoted to the delivery of food, medicine, and shelter when war is raging.

The more routine involvement by third-party military forces in humanitarian efforts is a remarkable phenomenon of the post-Cold War era – especially for Africa, where 70 percent of UN forces were deployed in 2012[37] – but the use of military forces for such purposes is not new. Although the earliest recorded instances date back centuries, a quantum expansion of the military into the humanitarian arena took place after World War II. The task of occupying Germany and Japan, as well as reconstructing as quickly as possible their economies, required new types of personnel within the armed forces: administrators, planners, and logisticians. At that time, of course, there were far fewer international NGOs, and the UN's humanitarian delivery mechanisms were just beginning to function.

In expanding the military's role as never before, military

assistance in natural disasters has become a routine extension of civil defense. Militaries, for instance, rush to the scene of national disasters but also overseas when monsoons and tsunamis strike, volcanoes erupt, or earthquakes tremble. Media treatment of these events has become commonplace since the dramatic involvement in humanitarian relief with the Berlin airlift of 1947, when an entire city was supplied. Fred Cuny wrote: "More than any other event, the images of those planes delivering everything from food to coal fostered acceptance of the link between armed forces and humanitarian assistance and, more importantly, acceptance of the costs incurred."[38]

Armed forces often possess an abundance of precisely those resources that are in the shortest supply when disaster strikes: transport, fuel, communications, commodities, building equipment, medicines, and large stockpiles of provisions. In addition, the military's "can-do" mentality, self-supporting character, rapid response capabilities, and its hierarchical discipline are essential assets within the turmoil of acute tragedies. Because both relief agencies and the public understand military resources and know-how, it is reasonable that political authorities think about calling upon its forces when local capacities have been overwhelmed by a disaster.

The second possible humanitarian benefit results from the military's direct exercise of security capacities, which is related to its primary function of war-fighting and using superior force to overwhelm hostile opponents. Such military humanitarianism should be carefully distinguished from military deployments after natural disasters or in tandem with traditional peacekeeping forces. Deployments for limited point relief during active armed conflicts, let alone large-scale humanitarian interventions, deploy military capabilities and assets for which there is no civilian substitute.

Such forces can gain access to suffering civilians, when insecurity makes it impossible or highly dangerous, and can foster a secure enough environment to permit their succor and protection. Such forces can also succeed in enforcing regime change that in turn permits civilian humanitarians to act. Critics have lambasted the security function because traditional humanitarians sometimes view "humanitarian intervention" and "humanitarian war" and especially the "humanitarian bombing" of Kosovo or Libya as oxymorons.[39] The potential political blow-back from body bags or from boots on the ground in never-ending humanitarian quagmires has led to something akin to a zero-casualty foreign policy for military efforts justified in basically humanitarian terms. Indeed, there was no genuine use of the military to protect human beings between 1999 (for Kosovo and East Timor) and 2011 (for Libya and Côte d'Ivoire). Nonetheless, the prevalence of what the ICISS blessed as "military intervention for human protection purposes" has become an integral component for the supply of humanitarianism and an important explanation for the size of the current marketplace. This development underpins many illustrations in subsequent chapters.

For-profit Firms

A brief discussion is merited of actors not commonly considered part of the international humanitarian system, PMSCs, and for-profit transnational corporations (TNCs).[40] Bad memories of colonial intrusion in the Third World have shaped perceptions of guns for hire, and international bodies have taken action to thwart such employment. Several international agreements have been reached: article 47 of Additional Protocol I to the Geneva Conventions of 1977;[41] the 1977 Convention for the Elimination of Mercenarism in Africa;[42] and the 1989 UN Convention against the Recruitment, Use, Financing, and Training of Mercenaries.[43] The UN also created the position of a special rapporteur to monitor developments and create guidelines in 1987, which was succeeded by a Working Group in 2005.[44] Furthermore, many national governments have legislation to ban mercenaries and regulate security firms.

Nonetheless, mercenaries and the more contemporary corporatized version of PMSCs are playing a growing role in contemporary war zones. Despite bans, mercenaries have appeared throughout the world, mostly in Africa but also in the Balkans, Latin America, and Southeast Asia. The war zones in which PMSCs tend to be deployed are also those in which international humanitarian law is typically ignored by belligerents – for example, PMSCs have had sizable operations in such diverse sites as Sierra Leone, Bogainville, and Borneo.[45] A well-publicized early case was the government of Sierra Leone's use of Executive Outcomes from 1995 to 1997 to repel insurgents who had been and were violating human rights on a massive scale. This experiment brought the possibilities for privately enhanced security to the agenda, and since then there has been mounting interest in the topic.[46]

In Afghanistan and Iraq, PMSCs became partners for regular military forces as well as for humanitarian organizations that contracted for their services. Few people realized that the US Defense Department had more contracted employees than troops in both countries; indeed, with troop withdrawals accelerating, the fatalities for contractors in Iraq were higher than for soldiers in 2011. Specific humanitarian tasks are subject to pressures to privatize. Budgetary as well as ideological influences have resulted in the increased use of private, market-based approaches for logistics, transportation, and security.

The belief that the private sector can provide services more cost-effectively than the public sector originally led to the increased use of multilateral organizations and NGOs rather than bilateral aid agencies; but the same logic spurred some donors to consciously funnel aid through for-profit channels rather than value-driven institutions. The spread of private corporations into what has conventionally been recognized as the domain of not-for-profit humanitarians can be viewed from supply and demand perspectives. On the demand side, the overwhelming dimensions of humanitarian needs figure prominently and are one reason for writing this book.

What about the supply side? In seeking to penetrate the market for humanitarian services, profit-oriented actors are engaged in recycling themselves. For example, doing "humanitarian" work allows Kellogg, Brown & Root, and DynCorp to emphasize their experience in rebuilding war-torn societies and economies rather than become bogged down with accounting for their ties to companies or parties sustaining or propelling conflicts. Building humanitarian credentials and capacities helps bottom lines.

Profit motives sometimes offend those with heartfelt charitable sentiments, and many humanitarians object on philosophical grounds to companies that profit from misery. But for-profit businesses are an alternative source of supply for succor.

Most private contractors are engaged in communications, transportation, and logistics. However, even more objectionable to many humanitarians are those private firms with significant military capabilities that are providing physical security, especially in the face of the unpredictable and widespread violence in such theaters as Afghanistan and Iraq. As humanitarianism has come to include physical protection for victims and aid workers, and as UN and state-based security resources are often unavailable or insufficient, private military companies are viewed as a possible option. Although the experience with "technicals" in Somalia (young men for hire with automatic weapons mounted on vehicles) was generally seen as a mistake, experiments began anew later in the 1990s and continue today that involve contracting PMSCs for humanitarian purposes.

Humanitarians have conventionally dismissed mercenaries. However, the idea of using private military contractors to provide protection or facilitate access for humanitarian agencies has gradually taken hold. Initially such a practice was seen as an extreme option. UN secretary-general Kofi Annan, for example, considered hiring a firm to disarm militants in Rwandan refugee camps when he was head of the Department of Peacekeeping Operations; however, he concluded that the contract would ignite political sensitivities, suggesting that the "world may not be ready" for private peacekeepers.[47] Subsequently, one study sponsored by Canadian NGOs in the aftermath of the international paralysis for the Rwandan genocide went so far as to recommend the creation of a private NGO army.[48] If governments were spineless, so the argument goes, why not privatize security so that outside humanitarians can come to the rescue? Accordingly, a few agencies made such arrangements, including World Vision in Sierra Leone and the UNHCR in Afghanistan.[49]

The use of PMSCs forces us to inquire who ultimately benefits politically and economically from humanitarian operations. Market-based versus principle-driven solutions highlight the difficulty of drawing lines between profit and predation. Without a profit margin, PMSCs would not sign contracts with humanitarian agencies. But as analysts such as Mark Duffield, Alex de Waal, and Michael Maren have shown, vulnerable people in many cases do not always receive the intended benefits of operations.[50]

What is the overall impact of privatization on the marketplace? Joanna Macrae points to "bilateralization," which consists of "a significant shift away from non-earmarked contributions to multilateral organizations in favor of more tightly earmarked grants, and a marked shift in favour of bilateral contracting with NGOs."[51] The result is less autonomy for IGOs and further uncertainty and market pressure on NGOs to toe the line or lose out. Rony Brauman, MSF's former head, wonders about the increased use of profit-making companies in Iraq to do what was previously the exclusive preserve of aid agencies: "Many NGOs fear that they will lose out to private companies, which are already claiming larger amounts of the 'NGO market,' and hence prefer to play the role requested of them to preserve their 'market share.'"[52] Based on a series of case studies in Iraq, Greg Hansen notes: "There has been a serious blurring of the lines in Iraq between military, political, not-for-profit and commercial actors, on the one hand, and humanitarian actors on the other hand, to the extent that many Iraqis (and some humanitarian professionals) cannot distinguish between the various sets of actors."[53] Ian Smillie and Larry Minear lament that "while the military and private contractors may make specific and indispensable humanitarian contributions ... the new breed is no substitute for the old."[54]

The boundary between expedient necessity and ethical booby trap has disappeared. With agencies operating in hostile and deadly environments, contracts for security arrangements with PMSCs have proliferated. What began as a trickle is becoming a flood. What are the implications for humanitarians and their traditional operating principles of independence, impartiality, and neutrality?

Answers to that question can be gleaned from two journalists reporting the sullied reputation of humanitarians in Afghanistan:

> They cannot reach parts of the country because of security threats. They are being blamed by many Afghans for the slow pace of reconstruction. They are accused of squandering funds on expensive cars and homes, and high salaries.

They are being confused with soldiers and private security contractors who carry weapons but wear civilian clothes. And they are being held accountable for the actions, or lack thereof, of numerous fly-by-night aid organizations seeking to cash in on Afghanistan's rebuilding.[55]

Contracts with for-profit organizations providing security suggest the need for critical reflections about the conditions under which subcontracts to for-profit firms can be justified. While substantial work has been done on transnational corporations and their networks and profits in war zones, the concern is mainly with cost effectiveness.[56] If the least costly and most effective supply of goods and services to vulnerable populations could be accomplished by a for-profit enterprise, should or would war victims care? If we take neoliberalism seriously, the existence of new resources has attracted new agencies, and so what is the problem with an emphasis on economic bottom lines? Why not open the competition as well to for-profit firms? While Michael Ignatieff praises the "revolution of moral concern," Stephen Hopgood asks questions about the "commodification of moral concern under globalization."[57]

This challenge finds its way into a provocative title from Hopgood, who pushes humanitarians to ask themselves honestly about the commodity of humanitarianism and thus whether or not they or recipients should be "Saying 'No' to Wal-Mart."[58] His answer is that humanitarians need to know what they do *and* why they do it. If humanitarian action is only a matter of delivery, then the case for calling upon Wal-Mart may be irresistible. In fact in 2006, the American Red Cross signed a disaster partnership with Wal-Mart, and the chief manager in the Florida Keys commented, "It's all going to private enterprise before it's over. They've got the expertise. They've got the resources."[59] If that logic applies to post-hurricane relief in Florida, is it not also pertinent in war zones?

If, however, humanitarians are following duty-based ethics (i.e., a moral obligation to help) or virtue-based ethics (i.e., the world will be a better place to live), they could justify and defend their value-added within the marketplace. That is, their focus on the victims rather than profits should be factored into the equation to determine the pluses and minuses of making a choice. However, they must do more than assert that it is morally repugnant to turn a profit in a war zone. In short, Hopgood believes that humanitarians could defend themselves because they reject "the logic of capital [which] is to make us see one another as partners in a variety of instrumental exchanges. The very logic of humanitarianism is to reject this idea precisely by helping those with whom no exchange is possible."[60] Whether that value-added is sufficient remains an open question.

The Media

The media are another type of for-profit business, although they traditionally have also had a public service role in informing citizens of facts and figures. In war zones, they can supply much-needed publicity and give voice to victims who might otherwise be silent. On numerous occasions their treatment of a crisis has led to the mobilization of political will to act and of resources to make a difference and save lives. To be sure, there were important precursors to what became the "CNN effect" or the "BBC effect,"[61] but real-time media coverage has continued as an important element of capturing the public's attention and stirring international action. The international media can pluck the heartstrings of outsiders to respond with assistance or push their elected officials to act and even to deploy military force.

We could begin with a popular current aphorism about the media coverage of wars, "if it bleeds it leads," but we should go back further in history. In 1917 US senator Hiram Warren Johnson noted that "the first casualty, when war comes, is truth," which acknowledges that warring parties as well as humanitarians also wage war with words and images. Media-savvy aid workers understand the power of images and the need to control information; and they spend considerable energy cultivating contacts with reporters and journalists. But as long as there have been nonprofit agencies, there have been dedicated staff who understand that a good public relations department and friends in the media increase the visibility and thus the donations that make organizations run.[62] In the nineteenth century, the media found opportunities to boost sales of newspapers by celebrating the spoils and raging against the injustices of war. There is doubt whether media mogul William Randolph Hearst actually promised to "furnish the war."[63] But when a reporter suggested there was no popular support for the 1898 Spanish–American War, the mainstream US media stoked this with slogans such as "Remember the Maine." The development and spread of radio captivated even a wider range of people hungry for news of wars.

Portraying humanitarian disasters has inherent difficulties: the press seeks the drama that makes for a good lead story; humanitarians hope for a message that opens pocketbooks; and analysts look for insights and truth in packaging about the nature of the costs and benefits of various factions. Narratives typically are laden with massive suffering and failed responses in visible disasters. How could the media portray a crisis that did not happen – that is, in which prevention was successful – or downplay the severity of violence or celebrate the success of non-heroic humanitarians?

Yet Andrew Natsios insists that we keep media influence in perspective. The director of USAID in the George W. Bush administration and of the Office of Foreign Disaster

Assistance in the George H.W. Bush administration and a vice president of World Vision in between argued that "the so-called CNN effect has taken on more importance than it deserves. . . . The truth is most complex emergencies get little media attention at any stage."[64]

Earthquakes, hurricanes, and tsunamis readily make headlines, but the cleanup following such ordeals is unlikely to be deemed newsworthy in light of the usual public attention deficit disorder. However, human-made emergencies are markedly different, especially when national or other important geopolitical interests are threatened. For those occasions, and especially if boots are on the ground, the media are pushing on an open door for a public keen about coverage. Even if such interests are absent, however, media attention may influence the availability of public and private funding. If a particular war zone is peripheral, the media will have an uphill battle to interest diplomats, the military, and parliamentarians.

Telling are the simple statistics regarding international responses to visible or "loud" emergencies versus those of invisible or "silent" emergencies. OCHA calculates total per capita resources available to victims of wars in various regions. When wars were raging in the Balkans, for instance, it was approximately 10 to 20 times more attractive to be a well-publicized victim in Europe than an almost invisible one in Africa.[65]

While gazing through the politicized media prism, three tiers of humanitarian crises can be distinguished: high-profile, visible, and forgotten. In the first instance, powerful geopolitical interests fuel humanitarian concerns, and agencies rapidly mobilize. Humanitarian interests are often conflated with political objectives. Proximity and the presence of troops make for powerful headlines and footage, as demonstrated by US troops in Somalia or Haiti in the 1990s or in Afghanistan or Iraq following the 9/11 attacks. In such crises, international media attention along with aid monies are abundant, leading to "limited absorptive capacity," or the inability of war-torn societies to make good use of the surfeit of resources that flow into high-profile emergencies.

The second level of war-related crises receive attention solely as humanitarian disasters but with no possibility for mustering military muscle or even adequate aid allocations. We can, for instance, point to such a crisis as Darfur in 2002–4: even as slow-motion genocide was taking place on camera and in headlines, there was more attention than resources. For such cases, states tend to substitute humanitarian action to cope rather than dedicate greater amounts of political and economic resources to address the larger issues, those that produced the crisis in the first place. The break-up of the former Yugoslavia and the first years of the accompanying emergency provide further illustrations. The "humanitarian alibi" in the Balkans seemed enough: why act militarily or politically when the application of the humanitarian salve was doing so much to lessen suffering?

The bottom tier consists of those emergencies with virtually no media or any other kind of attention. The long-standing disasters in Burma or northern Uganda, for instance, churn on in woeful anonymity. Media treatment fosters a narrative that such crises are unavoidable and waste resources, specifically implying that meaningful humanitarian action is impossible at best and foolish at worst.[66] The disappearance of Somalia from electronic and print media until a world-class famine broke out in 2011, in spite of substantial US military involvement earlier, suggests that action and media attention were out of sight and out of mind.

Fatigue – after two decades of a steady diet of covering humanitarian crises with print and pictures – is undoubtedly a problem for a journalist attempting to get stories of humanitarian needs in the DRC or Zimbabwe beyond the media's gatekeepers in editorial boards or editing rooms. Moreover, media coverage may also hurt the humanitarian impulse. "We cannot have misery without aid workers. They conjure away the horror by suggesting that help is at hand," writes Michael Ignatieff. "Coverage of humanitarian assistance allows the West the illusion that it is doing something; in this way, coverage becomes an alternative to more serious political engagement." He continues that the real story is thus one of disengagement "while the moral lullaby we allow our humanitarian consciences to sing is that we are coming closer and closer."[67] A similar comment comes from the BBC's Nik Gowing, who distinguishes between quality journalism and "noise" (different from "loud" emergencies that require in-depth treatment), which adds no analysis but, rather, "imperfect real-time reality."[68] John Hammock and Joel Charny have described the media's treatment as "a scripted morality play" whose simplified images contribute to compassion fatigue and a failure to educate the public and politicians about root causes.[69]

Hence, the conventional wisdom that media coverage drives policy and intervention – that is, "something must be done" – is usually off the mark. Images and coverage can be important in eliciting resources and galvanizing humanitarian responses when they align with or are nurtured by political power. How humanitarian crises and action are viewed matters – locally and internationally. Those deemed politically crucial receive the lion's share of attention and resources.

Media coverage can have negative as well as positive effects in the humanitarian marketplace. In specific instances where governments have virtually no direct interest – for example, Somalia was such a case in 1992 – the media can play an important role in "shaming" them and mobilizing publics to pressure elected officials to respond by publicizing the plight of civilians on the ground. In Somalia the coverage of war and famine mobilized international concern and responses (including by the US military). Afterwards, the dramatic images of US troops arriving on the beach in Mogadishu and Kismayo heightened American interest, but then the coverage of dead US Rangers accelerated the public's disaffection and the withdrawal of US and eventually UN troops.

In addition to dramatizing suffering and stimulating out-side action, the media can also contribute to generating the wrong messages and the wrong kinds of assistance; they can also skew allocations to high-decibel crises and away from low-decibel ones. The media can also overlook the role of local contributions, over-publicize the perceived bungling by humanitarians, and exaggerate the role of humanitarian relief to the detriment of solving underlying political negotiations and solutions.

Local Actors in the Marketplace

Turning to the war zone, it is important to underline actors that appear in Figure 1.1 and in all of the armed conflicts in this book: governments; insurgents; aid recipients; local nongovernmental organizations and other members of civil society; and businesses. Such local actors are generally less studied than the large international aid agencies discussed above, although local NGOs and businesses are recognized as an important part of the supply chain. UN, bilateral, and pri-vate organizations alike often rely on local actors, whether it is in the form of contracting for their services or buying neces-sary goods such as foodstuffs. Given their endogenous roots, local NGOs and businesses have a comparative advantage in communicating with recipient populations and may also pro-vide goods and services. Smaller and less financially resourced than their international counterparts, their knowledge of the language and customs of the suffering on the ground – or social capital – can make them indispensable, particularly in the acquisition and dissemination of information. As with other civilians in war zones, however, they are vulnerable to violence by belligerents, who may view any collaboration with international actors as antithetical to their interests.

While both the government and armed insurgents create the overall conditions and perpetuate violence that require outsiders and local humanitarians to come to the rescue, the belligerents can become part of the supply chain because they often have responsibility for the welfare of the people who live within the areas that they control. On the one hand, the pursuit of their war strategies and tactics savage individuals, groups, and entire civilian populations. On the other hand, belligerents also compete for the loyalty of people residing within areas that they control or seek to control. Thus, governments and armed insurgents have an obvious interest in ensuring that basic humanitarian needs are met in their respective strongholds because it strengthens their backing and standing. At the same time, they may obstruct humanitarian access to enemy areas. At a minimum, they are crucial "suppliers" of access as well as of "negative protection" – that is, by refraining from attacking civilians. They may also actually engage in service delivery. In the Ethiopian civil wars of the 1980s or Somali versions in the early 1990s or 2012, for example, the government and the armed opposition sought to assist some victims through official ministries or in comparable institutions with one or more insurgent movements to serve as channels for humanitarian resources.

Conclusion

Over the last few decades, the participants in the humanitarian business and indeed the marketplace have changed. Three transformative trends are apparent: militarization, politiciza-tion, and marketization. There are more boots on the ground from outside; providing aid entails making stark political choices with profound consequences for the well-being of war victims; and for-profit actors are gaining a greater foothold in what has become a lucrative business. Thus, in addition to the fact that there are more aid agencies than ever flocking to each crisis and taking on a spectrum of tasks beyond the delivery of life-saving assistance, the types of actors engaged in the humanitarian enterprise have diversified in terms of their organizational justifications. Both the military and PMSCs have a comparative advantage in the provision of physical pro-tection and crucial logistical services such as transport, which make them important actors in the delivery of relief in today's conflict contexts (and even in natural disasters).

As a result of contemporary transformations, civilian humanitarians are arguing among themselves about first principles – independence, impartiality, and neutrality – and undergoing something of an identity crisis in an increasingly competitive marketplace for humanitarian goods and serv-ices. We are now moving onto the often treacherous landscape on which humanitarians must provide succor to victimized populations. While delivering assistance to the suffering, humanitarians must now, more than ever before, be careful not to become victims of warfare themselves.

CHAPTER TWO

The Contemporary Landscape: Need and Greed

The turbulent winds swirling around the humanitarian suppliers, briefly alluded to in the preceding chapter, have led to a questioning of the relevance of "traditional" humanitarian action. This second chapter explores contemporary transformations in warfare and how they have had a direct impact on humanitarian practice. There also are three specific results that merit treatment in depth: growth in resources; increasing danger to aid personnel; and the uncomfortable truce between civilian aid workers and the military.[1]

New Wars

Among practitioners and analysts, one expression has come to dominate contemporary discourse: "new wars." Advanced by such scholars as Mary Kaldor and Mark Duffield as well as by such journalists as Robert Kaplan,[2] the catchy moniker can, however, lead to misunderstandings. It is less that totally new elements have appeared than that elements thought extinct or tangential have come to the fore or been combined in novel ways.[3]

More concretely, in comparing the older and newer varieties of armed conflict, we should delineate four essential changes. First, the locus of war no longer coincides with state borders; in areas of fragmented authority, in fact, borders often are meaningless. Second, instead of states and their militaries being the main agents, NSAs, increasingly, are critical protagonists. Third, the economies of war are no longer principally financed from local government tax revenues but rather from illicit activities, aid, and plunder. Fourth, instead of combatants being the main victims, civilians are paying the lion's share of costs, including fatalities.

While none of these four factors is totally unfamiliar to a student of warfare, the higher the number of significantly altered characteristics and the greater the quantity of change, the more an armed conflict merits the label "new." Whatever the adjective, the contemporary terrains are treacherous. Each factor should be dissected to determine how today's landscape differs from yesterday's and more precisely how it affects the marketplace.

The first and least disputed characteristic concerns the newness of the locus of war. The bloodiest wars of the first half of the twentieth century – including World War I and World War II – were waged by the regular armed forces of large and powerful states across borders for prolonged periods of time in order to gain territory, wealth, and influence. Other armed conflicts pitted a major power against a less powerful one that resisted, sometimes fighting for decolonization and sometimes manipulating rivals in a power struggle. However, whether it is France in Indochina, the United States in Central America, or the United Kingdom in the Falklands, defined borders and central government decisions still distinguished belligerents and defined these wars.

Why exactly are today's armed conflicts departures? One fundamental reason is that state parties tend to have minimal authority and power, and often even that is contested by multiple internal armed opposition movements that pay virtually no attention to internationally recognized borders or rules. Many countries have central governments whose existence mainly takes the form of UN membership and control of not much more than the capital city or the territory's main exports. These countries bear little or no resemblance to their more stable counterparts in the Westphalian order.[4] They exercise little or no authoritative control over populations and resources; and they certainly do not have a monopoly of the use of force. They suffer from an "unbundling" of territory from authority – a negation of exclusive authority as states.[5] Drug-crazed child soldiers who hack off the limbs of terrorized civilians in Sierra Leone capture some of the horror, as does the thought of seeking agreement from the forty or so armed opposition movements in the DRC, the new record-holder for numbers of insurgent groups as well as rape as a tactic for subjugation.

Max Weber and countless international relations scholars have emphasized the state's legitimate monopoly on violence and its authoritative position in society. However, much of the recent discussion of wars has instead focused on feeble relatives, on "weak" and "failed" states, which have been where humanitarian catastrophes have taken place, and where the complex humanitarian marketplace has functioned.

"Weak" describes states that do not measure up to Western or Third World role-models in international political prestige, wealth, military prowess, and national unity.[6] Such states typically lack the capacity to pursue national interests and are largely without an effective leader or bureaucracy.[7] They also usually lack the financial resources, technology, skill, or political capital to fulfill goals.

"Failed" states are weaker still. Gerald Helman and Steven Ratner coined the term in 1992 as Somalia imploded.[8] While "weak" suggests various vulnerabilities and capacities, "failed" implies a fatal illness in central authority – after 20 years of lurching from crisis to crisis, Somalia is still without anything resembling a central government. Not all weak states actually fail (e.g., Chad), and some collapsed ones can make a comeback (e.g., Lebanon).[9] While analysts contest the validity of the term, however, the image conveys how fundamental flaws destine a state to come apart at the seams.

Hedley Bull speculated in the 1970s about a possible return of violent sub-national contests over authority. In fact, international society and order have been jolted since the late twentieth century with unraveling state authority accompanied by huge humanitarian needs. Bull was unsettled by a potential "new medievalism,"[10] and the ugly reality has led scholars to draw parallels between today's wars and those that accompanied European state formation.[11] Mohammed Ayoob draws on Charles Tilly's work and argues against those who try to halt humanitarian emergencies by pointing out that armed conflict was an essential ingredient of eighteenth- and nineteenth-century European state-making, and that similar kinds of humanitarian disasters are the invariable by-product of comparable processes at work in much of the Third World.[12] It is hard to make an omelet, so the saying goes, without breaking eggs.

In short, as Kalevi Holsti reminds us, "the major problem of the contemporary society of states is no longer aggression, conquest and the obliteration of states. It is, rather, the collapse of states, humanitarian emergencies, state terror against segments of local populations, civil wars of various types, and international terrorist organizations."[13] Traditional humanitarian thinking may be based on unhelpful assumptions because the principles and tactics that worked well in the past for dealing with interstate wars are undoubtedly less useful in many of today's civil wars. One illustration of such problems, for instance, is that the de-institutionalization of sovereign central authority means a vastly diminished role for international humanitarian law.

The second defining characteristic of contemporary armed conflicts consists of the rise of unconventional political units, with dramatic implications for insecurity. For the past century, war has fundamentally been filtered through the lenses of state belligerents, which James Rosenau dubbed "sovereignty-bound" actors.[14] It should be clear that neither organized violence nor humanitarianism remains beholden only or even mainly to state authorities.

Some nonstate actors usurp the roles of states. Stephen Stedman and Fred Tanner use "pseudo-states" to denote crafty belligerents that manipulate the presence of refugees to attract and exploit humanitarian resources for their political gain.[15] Beatrice Hibou refers to criminal NSAs as "parallel states."[16]

While neither historically new nor completely absent from earlier interstate armed conflicts, the presence and scale of nonstate actors as political authorities and belligerents along with the inability of outside aid agencies in a growing number of crises to guarantee access constitute a new phenomenon. Three groups of NSAs are of particular concern. The first are armed belligerents: local militias, paramilitary groups, former military, or the followers of warlords. The second group are composed of those whose primary economic interests are served by violence. Ranging from mafia, criminal gangs, and illegal business to opportunistic profiteers, they may seek to sustain war and a humanitarian crisis, which promote an economic atmosphere conducive to their own profits.[17] The third group of "spoilers" – parties who believe that peace "threatens their power, worldview, and interests" and attempt to undermine its emergence[18] – consist of hybrids that blend military and economic agendas, mercenaries and private military companies.[19]

The third altered and salient characteristic of contemporary armed conflicts concerns the idiosyncratic economies of contemporary war zones that reflect unusual ways to make a profit. Many readers are no doubt familiar with Carl von Clausewitz's celebrated dictum that war is the continuation of politics, but David Keen argues that "war may be the continuation of *economics* by other means."[20] The economic conditions and structures of new wars permit individuals to pursue war and profits in new ways. When states are falling apart or putting themselves back together, unusual economic opportunities abound. Local balance sheets have always been important in fueling war, and certainly captains of industry from Krupp in the Third Reich to Halliburton in Iraq have been more than willing to help the national cause and simultaneously enrich corporate and personal coffers.

However, the local economy in contemporary wars plays a quantitatively and qualitatively different role than previously.[21] There is little production, mainly destruction. The economy and society as a whole suffer while isolated individuals benefit. With cash, arms, and power flowing into their hands, warring factions have no incentive to proceed to or remain at the negotiating table; instead, their interests are served by prolonging war and the accompanying economy that directly benefits them. The political economies of many contemporary wars mean that actors can concentrate their energies on controlling and illegally or legally exporting a few key resources like diamonds or tropical timber. Much spoiler behavior – before, during, and after wars – can be explained by their economic interests. In short, new wars present several opportunities for personal enrichment (protection and plunder) in addition to the prospects of an infusion of fungible resources from an aid economy.

Moreover, humanitarians provide additional elements for local profits because emergency aid itself has inadvertently contributed to fueling war. Not only does aid allow belligerents to pursue armed conflict by saving resources that they would otherwise spend on food or medicine, but its distributional impacts can also provoke violence.[22] Wars foster scarcity; and humanitarian assistance is a prize that can easily become an object for struggle among war's agents and victims.

Illustrations span the last few decades. In the late 1970s and 1980s, armed factions routinely vied for control of humanitarian assistance in refugee camps along the border between Cambodia and Thailand, a pattern currently being repeated in camps straddling the Afghanistan–Pakistan border.[23] Belligerents in Sudan (both government forces and the Sudan People's Liberation Army) used a variety of tactics to manipulate or monopolize aid: diverting aid, raiding staging areas, and feigning being noncombatants.[24]

Charity always seems worthwhile. But food, clothing, and shelter are fungible – that is, they can be used interchangeably with some of the resources used to fuel soldiers and war. Therefore, they can free other economic resources that can then be applied directly to the war effort rather than to keeping combatants or noncombatants alive. Moreover, humanitarian aid can be used to curry favor among supporters because elites receive credit for ensuring international assistance. If war is a good thing, why end it? War economies are such an important factor distorting the marketplace that we return to this topic in more detail in Chapter 4.

The fourth distinctive characteristic of contemporary armed conflicts is the prevalence of civilian casualties. The most extreme form is the intentional targeting of selected civilian populations – or genocide, the attempt to destroy entire populations because of their ethnicity or religion. But extermination of noncombatants is not the only strategy because forcibly displacing populations can accomplish many of the same heinous aims, which led to the coining of a new and disheartening euphemism, "ethnic cleansing." In the wars of the 1990s and 2000s, NSAs often operated without concern for humanitarian responsibilities and targeted populations, thereby producing an elevated toll of civilians killed in combat as well as dead from less direct but war-related causes like famine.[25]

Historically, civilians have always been targets. One analyst estimates that over the last three centuries they constituted about half of all war-related deaths.[26] What is unusual at present, however, is the extent to which civilian deaths are not by-products of violence but rather a central component of a successful military strategy. In the nightmarish trenches and surrounding areas in World War I (1914–18), 8.3 million soldiers and 8 million civilians died,[27] but the approximate 1:1 ratio of civilians to combatant casualties did not last. Despite fundamentally being an interstate conflict, World War II (1939–45) brought huge numbers of civilians into the fray: the German air blitz of London, the Allied fire-bombing of Dresden, atrocities perpetrated in Japanese-occupied Nanking and Manila, the Holocaust inflicted against European Jewry and other minorities, and ultimately the use of the atomic bomb by the United States against the residents of Hiroshima and Nagasaki. In the end, 23 million soldiers and over 57 million civilians lost their lives.

In retrospect, the 1:2.5 soldier:civilian ratio of casualties in World War II may seem mild today when civilians often represent an even more substantial percentage of war-related deaths. The Carnegie Commission was set up to find a way to prevent such violence and estimated that 90 percent of those killed in the new wars of the 1990s were civilians.[28] Mary Kaldor agrees with this trend, arguing that civilians accounted for 10–15 percent of total combat deaths at the start of the twentieth century, 50 percent during World War II (falling at the middle of the century), and 80 percent in new wars in the late 1990s.[29] Holsti's data depict a slightly sharper increase: only 50 percent of casualties were civilians in World War II, but in recent wars the figure is near 90 percent.[30] Virgil Hawkins goes even further and argues that civilians now constitute 95 percent of total combat deaths.[31]

Researchers continue to debate the precise ugly percentages, and many judge the alarmist statistics circulating widely as conventional wisdom to be wildly exaggerated and far from the mark.[32] Whatever the exact tally and however disputed the methodology, the crucial distinction for us here involves the motives for targeting civilians. The painful reality is clear: the "total war" associated with World War I was based upon the range of weapons permitted to be used against other soldiers. Today's ugly numbers may or may not involve a higher percentage of civilians, but wars now have a different "totality," comprehensive in the sense of routinely and specifically targeting civilians as part of the strategy and tactics of winning.

Not only local populations but also journalists and agency staff are targets. There are tactical and strategic reasons for taking aim at them. Tactically, humanitarian agencies may undermine nonstate actors by presenting an alternative source of vital resources to war-ravaged populations. Strategically, NSAs may also view attacking humanitarians as a means of signaling the seriousness of threats to outside military forces and governments. This topic is treated in more depth below because of its significance for those who toil in the humanitarian vineyards.

Paradoxically, positive normative developments to ensure access to and protection of vulnerable populations exist side-by-side with growing numbers of civilian victims – among populations as well as among those who come to their rescue or to report on the tragedy. The extent of this paradox reached new heights during the 1990s when atrocities with large numbers of civilian victims – in Iraq, Somalia, Bosnia, Rwanda, Kosovo, and East Timor – ultimately produced a dramatic shift in international political norms about intervening militarily to save lives. The parallel growth of norms and victims captures an ironic tragedy of the contemporary international order.

Humanitarian intervention is often necessary because

of the treacherous and unfamiliar terrain of the new wars – internal armed conflicts primarily waged by NSAs who subsist on illicit and parasitic economic behavior, use small arms and other basic hardware, and prey upon civilians, aid workers, and journalists. Since the end of the Cold War, new wars have ignited and cooled in many regions. And humanitarian intervention has played a role in helping – and, according to some critics, hindering – conflict resolution; and this too is discussed in depth later in the chapter.

As one might suspect, the new landscape of war has led to problems in pursuing humanitarian strategies and using humanitarian tactics developed for work on other terrains. We now turn to that topic.

The Politicization of Humanitarianism

Here we examine how contemporary civil wars not only strain the ability of humanitarian agencies to practically meet needs but also challenge their traditional operating principles: consent, impartiality, and neutrality. To begin, the scale of human suffering is mind-numbing. During the first decade of the post-Cold War era (1989 to 1999), wars (mainly civil but some international) killed over 1.5 million people and wounded and maimed countless others. More than fatalities and casualties, the number of people forcibly displaced by armed conflicts perhaps gives a better indication of the amplitude of the challenge for those coming to the rescue.

Although the numbers of people forcibly displaced have varied, over the last decade a good estimate at any moment was that approximately 1 in 135 of the world's population required international assistance and protection as a result of wars. In 2012, someone was forced to flee his or her home every eight minutes. According to the UNHCR, there are about 10.5 million refugees of concern to the agency, and an additional 4.5 million registered in 60 camps in the Middle East under the care of the UN Relief and Works Agency (UNRWA). The number of IDPs amounts to about double that of refugees – an estimated 28 million. And since 1992, according to the WFP, human-made food crises have doubled and now constitute 35 percent of the total that leave 90 million people in need across the globe.[33] These figures represent a very heavy burden for humanitarians, not to mention for war-torn societies themselves.

In addition to the staggering numbers of victimized populations in dire need of emergency provisions, such societies require multiple forms of assistance to avoid perpetual dependence on aid and the likelihood that their societies will relapse into armed conflict. This reality has generated questions about the very goals of agencies for the longer term. In today's armed conflicts, moreover, aid workers must grapple with thorny challenges merely to reach the suffering who urgently need their help. Later we discuss the heightened danger to the lives of humanitarians and various distortions in the local marketplace. Here, however, it is sufficient to indicate that humanitarians confront formidable dilemmas because their traditional operating principles are at best ineffective and at worst dysfunctional in war-torn areas. For instance, the UNHCR in its 2012 edition of *The State of the World's Refugees* admits, "When the principles are not fully respected yet action to meet vital needs still appears possible, humanitarian organizations may have to choose between bad and still worse options."[34] The transformation beginning in the late 1980s and early 1990s was variously described as "new humanitarianisms" and "political humanitarianism."[35] These labels point to a radical shift in both the humanitarian endeavor's social purpose and its fundamental operating principles.

Regarding social purpose, the traditional goal was straightforward: to save lives at risk through short-term assistance to belligerents and victims alike. Many agencies, however, have redefined the scope of their activities. Whereas they formerly saw their niche as temporary assistance, many began to design projects both upstream and downstream from the immediate violence of active warfare. They set aside their proclivity for short-term aid delivery in favor of both eliminating poverty and consolidating peace processes – inherently political processes.[36]

Humanitarians have thus become more brazen and ambitious. In light of the heart-wrenching experiences of the last two decades, the explanation may be found in the fact that relief workers continually fight a battle against despair and hopelessness. Would it not be helpful to believe that their devotion and action could also begin to alter the causes that give rise to the demand for their services in the first place? What could be more natural than wanting to believe that it is possible to build a new world? Or that human rights, conflict resolution, and nation-building should be viewed as extensions of humanitarianism?

For instance, from its founding through the civil wars of the 1980s, the UNHCR helped populations after they crossed an international border. Yet some staff bristled at this restriction, first extending helping hands to populations in "refugee-like situations" (i.e., IDPs) but then wanting to take on a more proactive role. As states became more niggardly about asylum, the UNHCR began trying to prevent refugee flows, to get at their "root causes," and to lobby for "state responsibility."[37] It was a small conceptual and bureaucratic step to become involved in eliminating the causes underlying the need to flee and ensuring that repatriated refugees stayed at home; next, however, the UNHCR began promoting human rights, the rule of law, and development. Humanitarianism's ambitions are understandably expansive; and its ethical slope is quintessentially slippery – well-intentioned people naturally want to do more.

The shift from emergency relief to attacking root causes and post-conflict peace-building represents an ambitious agenda. No longer satisfied with saving individuals today to place them in jeopardy tomorrow – the infamous "well-fed dead" is a memorable framing about aid in the former Yugoslavia by Fred Cuny,[38] who was allegedly executed by Chechen rebels in April 1995 – many humanitarians now aspire to nothing less than improving the structural conditions that endanger vulnerable populations. Rather than applying salve and band-aids, they wish to use assistance and protection as levers to spread development, democracy, and human rights and to create stable, effective, and legitimate states.[39]

As humanitarians have attempted to promote human rights, they have found that neutrality can be an obstacle. Similarly, consent and impartiality have been called into question. Traditional principles are framed by the logic of the interstate system and thus are untenable in many civil wars. Indeed, they may actually be dysfunctional. Once a state ceases to maintain political authority or to have a monopoly on violence, borders lose meaning. The focus of today's conflicts on people or resources more than on territory or formal boundaries creates a disconnect when humanitarians respond to conflicts that cross borders but are obliged to seek consent from territorially defined belligerents. UN organizations are bound by their constitutions to interact with member states, and NGOs have usually operated in a similar fashion even if their terms of incorporation are not circumscribed by national boundaries. State belligerents were also the guarantors of humanitarian space – room to maneuver and help in providing protection and relief to war-ravaged populations – which is codified in the Geneva Conventions.[40]

Moreover, in situations where the state is under stress or

is nonexistent, agencies are on dubious legal ground, and this uncertainty not only carries over but also is multiplied for arrangements with nonstate actors. There are only a few references in international humanitarian law – basically in common Article 3 to the Geneva Conventions and Article 1 of Additional Protocol II. Negotiations previously centered on state authorities. However nebulous or cumbersome the procedures, at least the channels or the official interlocutors were clear. To the extent that wars no longer follow the contours of borders and shift onto more uncertain political, economic, and social terrain, agencies have no choice except to widen the range of actors with whom they negotiate access to affected populations.

Areas lacking central state authority but containing menacing NSAs thus create tremendous difficulties in accessing victims. In contemporary armed conflicts, aid agencies often do not benefit from the luxury of the Geneva Conventions. Indeed, belligerents often do not provide consent, allow for the passage of relief, or respect international agreements – in fact, they are often unaware of them and are not signatories. Hence, the most elementary struggle is for aid agencies to carve out secure space in which to operate. One option has been to cooperate with intervening militaries that force open space in war zones to reach victims, a practice that began with northern Iraq in the early 1990s when the Security Council first authorized the creation of a safe area without the consent of the government – indeed, it did so against its expressed wishes.[41] When belligerents "commodify" access – that is, when they attach a price to it – another option for agencies emerges: to pay for it.

Impartiality also made sense when the objective was to provide relief and gain access to affected populations and when combatants were from state militaries and usually respected the laws of war. In the wake of the Rwandan genocide, many humanitarians – and donors who paid the bills – recognized that even the best efforts were producing unexpected and pernicious results. Being apolitical in the distribution of assistance is indefensible when it produces what economists call "negative externalities" – that is, costs not reflected in a product – for already victimized populations. In the case of Rwanda, aid strengthened the position of the genocide's perpetrators, who had fled to Zaïre and controlled camps there. Unintended negative consequences meant that reciting the humanitarian mantra was of little avail; the former guidelines in the form of traditional principles provided no or even bad guidance. In yet another recent reversal of his earlier views, David Rieff tells us that "humanitarian space is a sentimental idea, neutrality a bogus one, and impartiality an abstraction. . . . The sooner they are given a decent burial, the sooner we can all move on."[42]

In short, transformations in warfare are reshaping humanitarian practice. Operational principles intended to insulate agencies from politics are untenable on the ground in today's armed conflicts. The collective learning curve has been steep. From the founding of the international humanitarian system through the final stages of the Cold War, humanitarian action was predicated upon state consent and support.[43] In civil wars where the state is weak or nonexistent, war is privatized and fed by illicit markets, and civilians themselves are targets; standard operating procedures are not only ineffective at alleviating suffering but actually can cause further harm to war victims – as so starkly illustrated in Bosnia and Rwanda.

In order to cope with the causes and scope of crises that became more common beginning in the 1990s, agencies are slowly shedding the system's interstate logic. The specific actions and policies of certain agencies such as MSF and the UNHCR were instrumental in pushing the political envelope of humanitarianism by making choices that would reverberate throughout the international system. Increasing work with NSAs and sometimes without the consent of belligerents revealed the politics upon which the system hinges.

Resources, Risks, and Trade-offs

Today's changed landscape is prompting transformations in the humanitarian sector in terms of the resources, risks, and trade-offs of relying on outside militaries to assist in the delivery of aid and the protection of civilians, including humanitarians themselves. This section first discusses in depth the growth of financial resources both from states and from the private sector. The availability of funds for humanitarian action used to be basically financed by government resources in donor countries coming from public budgets and directed toward recipient states. The "double monopoly" of state control has been replaced by a remarkable diversification of both demand and supply of humanitarian monies. The section then examines the increased risks for civilian personnel and finally the trade-offs of relying on military or private security actors in the humanitarian endeavor.

Growth in Resources

Within weakening or collapsing states, outside agencies have become the main life-line for distressed populations and have replaced and sometimes eroded traditional coping capacities. This growth in dependency is tragic for those societies and overwhelming for outsiders providing succor; and it bodes ill for post-conflict peacebuilding.[44] Among the top 10 recipients of international humanitarian aid between 2000 and 2009 were Sudan, Palestine, Iraq, Afghanistan, Ethiopia, the DRC, and Somalia. The *Global Humanitarian Assistance (GHA) Report 2011* classified 18 of the top 20 as "conflict-affected" countries. Fifteen were classified as "long-term recipients."

The report also noted that humanitarian financing has indeed become increasingly concentrated in conflict-affected states, rising from less than 40 percent in 2000 to 65 percent in 2009.[45]

As discussed in the previous chapter, established institutions have increased in size and scope while new agencies have sprung up as the need for humanitarian services has grown. Here the focus is on the rapid growth in the resources of IGOs and NGOs, which has been unprecedented – over a five-fold increase in humanitarian aid in the first post-Cold War decade, from about $800 million in 1989 to some $4.4 billion in 1999.[46] The upward trend continued, with estimates reaching a quadrupling to $16.7 billion in 2010.[47]

The funds flowing into and circulating within the humanitarian business are thus substantial. Much of this funding has been channeled through the UN system and about a half dozen or so of the largest NGOs. In 2009, about 62 percent of the $12.1 billion in funding traceable through the humanitarian aid system was channeled through multilateral mechanisms, while 17 percent went directly to NGOs, 9 percent to the International Red Cross and Red Crescent Movement, and less than 10 percent through bilateral agencies. The top five multilateral recipients of aid monies were the WFP, UNHCR, UNRWA, UNDP, and OCHA. Although robust data are not available on the funds that NGOs receive through UN agency contracts, international NGOs controlled almost 40 percent of pooled humanitarian funds in 2010, amounting to about $134 million.[48] As mentioned earlier, it is the strings attached and the priorities dictated by bilateral donors that account for *de facto* "bilateralization" even if more resources now are flowing through nongovernmental and multilateral executing agencies.

There is more money for humanitarian action than ever before, largely thanks to states and taxpayers. Over the past decade, governments have spent an estimated $90 billion on humanitarian assistance. In 2010, alone they provided $12.4 billion, while private voluntary contributions reached $4.3 billion, up from $2.7 billion in 2006. In 2009, moreover, UN peace operations amounted to $9.1 billion, and most of these soldiers were in the same countries receiving civilian humanitarian aid.

These figures, of course, underestimate the total figure, as they exclude the efforts of crisis-affected countries themselves and military responses to crises. As UN high commissioner for refugees António Guterres notes, "Local communities often demonstrate a remarkable willingness to share their land, water, forest resources, as well as their health and education services with strangers who have fled from man-made and natural disasters."[49] Neighbors and neighboring areas or countries often support or harbor people who have fled wars, but such help is rarely recorded. Friends and family members living outside the war zone may send remittances, but they are private and thus not subject to international accounting. Both for-profit firms and the military – from the affected area as well as from outside it – give humanitarian aid; but unless they are channeled through NGOs or reported to the UN's Financial Tracking System (FTS), most such contributions are overlooked. Also, there is a fair bit of private religious giving that does not go through the "system." For instance, there are more mega-churches than ever before with their own missionary and social action arms; and so when emergency strikes, they have the opportunity to give directly to affected communities rather than going through established NGOs or the United Nations. Indeed, in what Michael Barnett and Janice Stein call "the third wave of globalization," what jumps out is "the growth in both transnational religious activism and humanitarianism from outside the West."[50]

Considerable   debate   surrounds   whether   short-term, life-saving, and exceptional humanitarian aid is growing at the expense of longer-term development assistance. As the 2009 *Global Humanitarian Assistance* report points out, "the majority of humanitarian assistance over the past 13 years has been spent on long-term, protracted crises in countries that are classified as 'chronically poor.'"[51] Humanitarian and development assistance are growing closer together, or perhaps such distinctions are irrelevant in a large number of cases.

Moreover, as a proportion of official development assistance (ODA), humanitarian aid rose from an average of around 6 percent in the early 1990s to somewhere between 7.5 and 10 percent over the 1990s.[52] Over a longer period, total ODA has shrunk, but the humanitarian component has continued to grow. "From 1970–1990 humanitarian aid was less than 3% of total ODA," calculated a team from the Overseas Development Institute, "while ODA . . . as a whole has been declining as a share of donor countries' national wealth or Gross National Income (GNI), humanitarian ODA has been growing. In 1970 DAC [Development Assistance Committee] member countries gave 0.4 of a cent in humanitarian aid for every $100 in national income. In 2001 it was 2.3 cents."[53] *GHA Report 2011* estimates that humanitarian aid has constituted 8.7 percent of Organization for Economic Co-operation and Development (OECD)/DAC ODA expenditure since 2000.[54]

A few donors were responsible for much of this increase. In spite of its miserly performance at the bottom of the OECD's per capita ODA scale, the United States is the lead humanitarian country donor. Between 2000 and 2009, it provided more than 30 percent of aggregate humanitarian assistance from governments, about double the figure for the next top contributor, and almost four times the third largest donor. In 2010, the United States contributed about 35 percent of total government contributions. The second largest donor remains the

European Union, followed by the United Kingdom and several other European countries; indeed, the EU and European countries together now account for 50 percent of aid totals worldwide, and probably a similar portion of humanitarian assistance totals. Canada and Japan are also important sources. While some diversification has taken place, the vast bulk of humanitarian resources continue to emanate from the West, with alternative sources hovering around 10 percent of the total in any year.[55]

Although the West continues to dominate the numbers, more and more governments are responding to disasters of all sorts. For example, whereas 16 states pledged their support to Bosnia in the mid-1990s, most from the West, a more diverse group of 73 attended the 2003 pledging conference in Madrid for Iraq, and an unprecedented 92 responded to the December 2004 tsunami. One overview of recent trends summarized the current situation as follows: "From as few as a dozen government financiers just over a decade ago, it is now commonplace to see 50 or 60 donor governments supporting a humanitarian response."[56] In 2009, 107 governments figure on a composite list of contributors to the international humanitarian response to crises.[57] While OECD's DAC governments almost doubled their assistance between 2000 and 2010 from $6.7 billion to $11.8 billion, non-OECD DAC governments increased their contributions from $35 million to $623 million[58] – almost an 18-fold increase, albeit from a much lower base.

Such important non-Western donors as China, Saudi Arabia, India, and the United Arab Emirates have accounted for up to 12 percent of official humanitarian assistance in a given year; and their influence in certain crises – for example, Afghanistan or Palestine – is even more significant. Most of the countries that are not members of the OECD's DAC concentrate their aid on neighboring countries; and the vast bulk of such assistance (over 90 percent or almost $1 billion in 2008) emanates from the Gulf states. In fact, Saudi Arabia accounted for three-quarters of the non-OECD/DAC sum and was the third largest humanitarian donor in the world that year.[59] Along with the United Arab Emirates and Kuwait, these states now account for larger humanitarian expenditures than some of the smaller Western countries. In 2009, the United Arab Emirates ranked third in generosity on a per person basis. At the same time, MSF's private voluntary contributions alone in 2010, amounting to $1.1 billion, outstripped all non-traditional sources combined and even rivaled the United Kingdom – the third largest donor.[60]

We know precious little about whether non-traditional donors follow the major Western states in their rationales and their prioritization for policy options.[61] But non-traditional donors are more likely to channel their donations through the public sector (of both the recipient and donor countries) and the ICRC but give relatively little to NGOs. They resemble their OECD counterparts in preferring bilateral aid or tied aid to proximate countries in their regions; they too are using their financial support as a political tool to increase their influence. Nonetheless, the international humanitarian business mainly operates with funding from North America and Western Europe, accounting for about $11.8 billion of the total $12.4 billion of official humanitarian assistance in 2010.[62]

In short, while non-Western donors have entered the market with more aid than ever before, the vast bulk of resources is still controlled by a few Western countries that are inclined to impose conditions and channel aid toward their priorities. While funding according to need has always supposedly guided humanitarians and is a fundamental principle subscribed to by DAC donors, there is little uniformity in their performance. We would agree with Hugo Slim that the humanitarian enterprise "works wherever it can in international society but is not really owned by all of international society."[63]

Increasing Danger

Humanitarian workers and war correspondents increasingly find themselves in the cross-hairs of weapons aimed specifically at them. The present moment can certainly be distinguished from earlier ones by the risks to aid personnel.[64] In the first decade of the twenty-first century alone, over 200 civilian UN staff (i.e., not including military peacekeepers, whose fatalities were actually lower) died in almost 50 countries, and another 300 were taken hostage. The ICRC lost some 50 staff members. One study of the impact of firearms on aid workers notes that "between July 2003 and July 2004 at least 100 civilian UN and NGO personnel died due to targeted violence."[65]

Afghanistan and Iraq skewed the numbers regarding fatalities of civilian personnel. In Afghanistan, at least 26 aid-agency staff died in 2004 alone.[66] Even the intrepid MSF decided that enough was enough and withdrew after five staff were murdered there in mid-2004. Later, three insurgents dressed as police scaled a fence at the UN guesthouse in northern Afghanistan and killed five UN staff in a two-hour gun battle. August 2010 witnessed the grisly execution of 10 medical personnel working in the eastern province of Badakhshan for the International Assistance Mission. The best publicized of such cowardly assaults took place earlier in Iraq in 2003 and shook humanitarians to the core: the August 19 attack on the UN headquarters in Baghdad that resulted in 22 fatalities, including the charismatic head of the mission, Sergio Vieira de Mello; and six weeks later, a car bomb delivered in a white ambulance painted with a red-crescent symbol that killed 15 at the ICRC's country headquarters.

And the list goes on in other theaters as well. In August

2006, for example, 17 staff from Action Against Hunger were brutally murdered in Sri Lanka; and their deaths were especially shocking because they were in the right place at the wrong time – specifically to help in post-tsunami relief and not the civil war between the Sri Lankan army and the Tamil Tigers. Another brazen attack shook the aid establishment in October 2009: five WFP staff died after a suicide attack in the program's offices in Islamabad. According to the April 2011 OCHA report, *To Stay and Deliver*, the number of attacks against aid workers has tripled over the first decade of the twenty-first century, with an estimated 100 deaths per year. Unsurprisingly, war-torn Afghanistan, Somalia, and Sudan headed the list, with fatalities in these countries inflating global trends.[67]

Following the deaths of 17 staff in an attack on the UN headquarters in Algiers in 2007, the former Algerian foreign minister and veteran UN handyman Lakhdar Brahimi was asked to chair the Independent Panel on Safety and Security of United Nations Personnel and Premises. The report's clear message was: the UN blue flag no longer provides any safety – in fact, it seems to have become a target.[68] "The simple truth is that humanitarian workers are no longer, if they ever were, shielded from violence and attacks of various forms by the mere fact of being in the humanitarian field. Quite the contrary," a former UNHCR official tells us, "they are now sometimes deliberately targeted because they are humanitarians."[69] In many war-torn societies with Muslim majorities, such as Afghanistan and Iraq, the UN has come to be perceived as serving the interests of the major powers, sometimes even as an appendage to the occupying forces. It is seen as applying a double standard by using force against them while doing virtually nothing to enforce long-standing resolutions in favor of Palestinians against Israel.

Jan Egeland arrived in New York for his briefing as UN

under-secretary-general for humanitarian affairs on the very day that the world organization's Baghdad headquarters was destroyed. He noted the irony in his memoirs of the period: "The age of innocence has gone. . . . I had expected to spend all my energies in the UN on the security and survival of disaster and conflict victims, not the security and survival of our own UN staff."[70] Shortly thereafter, *The Economist* opined, "It was not until the American-led wars in Afghanistan and Iraq that the UN and other aid agencies began to be deliberately hunted down."[71]

That view was undoubtedly something of an exaggeration, but the spate of highly visible individual episodes led to a debate about whether the vulnerability of aid workers has actually increased in recent years. The beginning of an evidence-based response came in the form of the first thorough quantitative analysis of trends for the new wars and new humanitarianisms. The absolute number of attacks and fatalities indeed doubled between 1997 and 2005, but the increase reflected the presence of more aid workers and projects than ever before as part of the humanitarian business. Specifically, "the annual number of victims per 10,000 aid workers in the field averaged five in the first half of the period and six in the second." There is also some evidence that NGOs were more likely to be targeted, but with considerable variation, and that Afghanistan and Iraq are outliers distorting the average. In the update of these statistics in 2009, Abby Stoddard, Adele Harmer, and Katherine Haver found that attacks had increased sharply over 2006–8 – almost a doubling in deaths and kidnapping from the previous three years – with rates being especially bad for NGO expatriate staff and UN local contractors. Three conflicts (Darfur, Afghanistan, and Somalia) accounted for about 60 percent of the violence and victims.[72] An update that covered 2005–10 showed that these war zones still led the list, followed closely by Sri Lanka,

Pakistan, the DRC, Iraq, and occupied Palestine. During the decade ending in 2010, almost 800 aid workers lost their lives.[73]

The debate about danger ultimately turns around the extent to which Afghanistan and Iraq are aberrations or rather a "model" for the future. Journalists, for instance, would certainly see Iraq as quite a "new" level of threat to their profession: covering the war has assumed its place as the deadliest conflict for reporters in modern times. In a little over two years following the start of the war in March 2003, 73 journalists lost their lives covering that conflict – more than the 66 killed in Vietnam and the 68 in all theaters during World War II.[74] According to a 2010 report by Reporters without Borders, an astounding 230 media staff, 172 of whom were journalists, died in Iraq in the previous seven years.[75]

In earlier periods, the humanitarian mantle had afforded meaningful physical protection, but the danger to and the loss of personnel during the new wars has prompted humanitarians to push for legal protection. In the early 1990s, the Security Council noted the increased violence directed toward aid workers. During humanitarian operations in Somalia in 1993, the council passed resolution 814 to respond to "acts of violence against persons engaging in humanitarian efforts." Shortly thereafter the UN also adopted a convention criminalizing attacks on such international personnel that entered into force in January 1999.

Perhaps the grimmest examples can bring home why the continuation of humanitarian business-as-usual is not an option. The videotaped beheading of the *Wall Street Journal's* Daniel Pearl in January 2002 was gruesome enough. But the ceremonial murder in November 2004 of CARE's Iraq country director, Margaret Hassan, was an undoubtedly calculated way to shake humanitarians to the core. Having lived in the country for thirty years and married a Muslim Iraqi did not make her less vulnerable; in fact, she was the perfect symbolic target who could transmit a chilling message about insecurity for *all* foreigners no matter what their background, dedication, or commitment.

Much outrage in the West tends to focus on expatriate aid workers when, in fact, a growing percentage of agency personnel are drawn from vulnerable local populations who are hired by outside agencies – a recent survey suggests that only 7 percent of personnel in war zones are internationals.[76] Probably 80 percent of casualties and fatalities among the staffs of Western aid organizations are nationals from the country being assisted.[77] Indeed, to the extent that Western aid workers remove or distance themselves from the field, risk may be shifting toward locally recruited workers. In any case, aid personnel can no longer assume (if they ever could) that their good intentions give them immunity.[78]

Moreover, the "performance" value of the violent attacks on humanitarians appears quite new, especially in contexts like Afghanistan and Iraq where locals working for aid agencies may be perceived as "collaborators."[79] Anthropologist Laura Hammond examines such gruesome theaters and finds that "attacking humanitarian organizations is intended to be a symbolically potent act, a purposeful rejection of humanitarian principles and the self-righteous claim that aid providers lay to those principles." In arguing that such violence should be seen as part of military strategy, she understands that subverting humanitarianism "becomes a powerful way of sending a message not only to civilians trapped in the conflict but also to those living in safer places who might be in a position to offer their public, material, or financial support to the war effort."[80]

Today's complex emergencies mean that civilian humanitarians may not be able to base their staff in a country in distress. They may have little choice but to rely on local contractors to monitor hundreds of millions of dollars of aid deliveries. When civilian staff are kept at safe distances, supplies are more vulnerable to theft. Corrupt businessmen, sometimes in collaboration with warlords and militants, have been known to loot the aid that they have been hired to oversee, which is then sold on the open market at a profit. The practice is so standard that it has come to be known as "traditional distribution" – the siphoning off of aid as a cost to help suffering populations. As one aid official noted, in Somalia during the early 1990s, 10 to 15 percent of seepage was "the price of doing business."[81] Two decades later, the WFP's food is again being stolen to serve private interests rather than feed the war-ravaged and famine-stricken Somalis whom it is intended for.

Trade-offs of Militarized Humanitarianism

The dramatic increases in the numbers and kinds of civilian fatalities and human rights abuses heightened calls by humanitarians themselves for military resources to help protect victims and ensure access by humanitarians. In the context of war zones where belligerents target aid workers and serve as gatekeepers, there may be no alternative to military assistance and protection.

It would be useful at this juncture to parse the use of outside military force. The two end-points on a spectrum of outside assistance are relatively well understood. Traditional peacekeeping is based on the principles of consent, neutrality, and the non-use of force except in self-defense. This form of military deployment is designed to create and maintain conditions in which political negotiations can proceed – in effect, to monitor compliance with an agreement to which belligerents have committed themselves. It involves patrolling buffer zones between hostile parties, monitoring cease-fires, and helping defuse local spats. Ongoing examples of traditional peacekeeping include unarmed military observers in Western Sahara and armed infantry in Cyprus. On the other end of the spectrum lies the equally well-understood concept of war-fighting. Here the objective is to defeat a clearly defined adversary, and it is undertaken by fully combat-capable troops. The North Atlantic Treaty Organization's (NATO) air campaigns of 1999 in Kosovo and 2011 in Libya fall into this category.

However, over the course of the 1990s, activities falling between these two extremes became a common yet highly controversial form of international military operations. Here it is useful to distinguish between two related but quite distinct sets of objectives: compelling compliance and providing protection. The former, commonly referred to as "peace enforcement," involves the search for comprehensive political settlements leading to sustainable peace. It entails traditional peacekeeping tasks such as monitoring cease-fires, but it also encompasses more complex ones whose ultimate success requires a willingness and a capacity to use deadly force. These include the "cantonment and demobilization of soldiers; the destruction of weapons; the formation and training of new armed forces; [and] monitoring existing police forces and forming new ones."[82] Examples of this form of military operation include NATO's Implementation Force and Stabilization Force in Bosnia, and the US-led Multinational Force in Haiti. A variant on this approach is the use of force to compel parties to negotiate. The 1995 NATO air-strikes on Bosnia preceding the Dayton Accords are an example.

The other form of enforcement action consists of providing protection for civilians backed by the threat or use of military force. While "coercive protection" can take a variety of forms, the most common are the maintenance of humanitarian corridors, the protection of aid convoys, and the creation of safe havens or protected areas. Prominent examples include the no-fly-zone in northern Iraq and the so-called safe areas of Bosnia. A particularly important dimension of this kind of operation is the force posture of intervening troops. Coercive protection is distinct from the other military operations, which have military forces positioned in relation to opposing military forces. Peacekeeping involves monitoring military cease-fires or interposing forces between armed parties to the conflict; compelling compliance involves the potential use of force against conflicting parties or spoilers; and war-fighting involves combat against designated opponents.

In contrast, the provision of protection requires the inter-position of forces between potential attackers (armies, militias, and gangs), on the one hand, and noncombatant civilians, on the other hand. The responsibility to protect civilians presents many challenging tasks that are not favored by militaries around the world. They are the forcible disarmament of belligerents (especially in refugee camps like those in eastern Zaïre); the meaningful protection of safe areas (the gruesome example of Srebrenica comes immediately to mind); and the protection of humanitarian workers. The unsettling images of bombed-out UN and ICRC headquarters in Iraq are hard to forget when a UN soldier is advised to turn the other cheek.

Throughout these pages, readers encounter differing views about the pluses and minuses of using outside military force to protect human beings who are caught in the throes of the new wars. There has been little consistency in views among humanitarians over time. Indeed, sometimes "NGOs were more gung-ho than the soldiers were."[83] The ICRC, for instance, as the custodian of the laws of war, traditionally has kept its distance from soldiers. However, in the chaos of Somalia, it experimented with hiring "technicals." Its president during the tumultuous 1990s, Cornelio Sommaruga, was a member of ICISS and insisted that his fellow commissioners set aside the expression "humanitarian intervention"

and use instead "military intervention for human protection purposes." Prize-winning journalist David Rieff was an
enthusiastic proponent of armed intervention in the Balkans
and Rwanda but thereafter did an about-face as he found himself and "humanitarianism in crisis." Disillusioned with what
he found in war zones, he proposed returning to the "good
old days" of neutral and impartial aid without the use of military humanitarianism.[84] Changing his stance once again,
Rieff has subsequently argued that aid is inherently political
and the sooner we dispel the myth the better.[85] As two observers note: "There is no 'golden age' of humanitarian space but
rather periods in which humanitarian action was frequently
and deeply politicized."[86]

Relying on the military in a particular humanitarian crisis
creates dilemmas for humanitarians. On the one hand, the
military can force open space and thus allow agencies to reach
the suffering. The military can also protect war victims and
humanitarians themselves. On the other hand, it presents a
danger that might overwhelm aid agencies.

The use of military force necessarily clashes with the traditional principles of the independent, neutral, and impartial
provision of relief to victims of armed conflict. As such, relief-
oriented actors who dishonor that definition may be perceived
by belligerents as working against their interests. In its most
extreme form, which many see in the actual experiences in
Afghanistan and Iraq, humanitarians who collaborate with the
military can be seen to embody colonialism and imperialism
as an extension of the occupying military force.

In terms of the actual delivery of assistance, the military
may have superior logistical capacity, but in collaborating with
them humanitarian agencies may lose autonomy in terms
of decisions about how and where to distribute aid that are
consistent with their organizational priorities and principles.
The military logistics cornucopia should also be considered

in parallel with the adequacy of funds for civilian humanitarian agencies – is military humanitarianism an addition to or a replacement for civilian efforts? The public perception is that the costs of military participation in humanitarian exercises are borne by respective military establishments. But in many, perhaps most, countries, defense ministries are reimbursed totally or in part for their contributions from the budgets of foreign ministries or aid departments. Even when the military is not reimbursed, developing an overall program to address a particular emergency normally reflects conscious choices between military and civilian entities competing for limited funds.

Contracting private security companies creates a different set of problems. Utilizing actors with ulterior motives – that is, profit – can distort operations, alienate victims, and undermine the reputation of civilian humanitarians. The security that PMSCs provide to aid convoys and workers can be costly. Resources spent in this way necessarily are subtracted from funds for food and other supplies.

Private contractors occupy a murky legal position in the marketplace. In relationship to international humanitarian law, PMSCs do not conform to the prototype of a mercenary, and debate continues regarding whether they fall under Article 47 of Additional Protocol I. The Fourth Geneva Convention concerns noncombatants, which may not apply to contractors who are armed. The Third Geneva Convention governs prisoners of war but may not apply either because contractors operate without uniforms and do not adhere to formal military chains of command. The rules for personnel who service troops on military bases are defined, but those governing personnel who fight in the shadows (e.g., chasing the Taliban and Al-Qaeda on the Afghanistan–Pakistan border) are unclear.

Whatever the economic advantages, former UN special rapporteur on mercenaries Enrique Ballestros suggests that using PMSCs has distressing implications for human rights: "Mercenaries base their comparative advantage and greater efficiency on the fact that they do not regard themselves as being bound to respect human rights or the rule of IHL [international humanitarian law]. Greater disdain for human dignity and greater cruelty are considered efficient instruments for winning the fight."[87] Furthermore, instances have occurred in which a contractor performing a security task with humanitarian implications had employees who were later implicated in sex trafficking.[88] In Bosnia in 1999, for example, employees of DynCorp, a US-based security contractor, engaged in child prostitution and the sex trade. About a decade later, DynCorp was in the news again with allegations that foreign employees based in Afghanistan had taken drugs and paid young "dancing boys" to entertain them – an incident that came on the heels of Blackwater's accidental killing of civilian Afghanis.[89]

Despite the range of potential political and legal problems, the warming relationship between the humanitarian and private military sectors is noteworthy, especially in Afghanistan and Iraq,[90] although Somalia "has the highest percentage of humanitarian organisations using armed protection to run their operations."[91] The intense hostility and fear that gripped humanitarians has loosened to the point where mainstream agencies have dropped many of their usual reservations; and in fact, some have hired PMSCs. Claude Voillat, from the ICRC's relations with the private sector unit, notes, "Up to now, contacts between the ICRC and private military and security companies have taken place on an informal basis. The ICRC now plans a more systematic approach focusing on companies operating in conflict situations or providing training and advice to armed forces." Furthermore, the Red Cross accepts that private solutions to security problems are here to stay and that the focus of agencies should be on regulating armed actors. "The ICRC does not plan to take a position on the legitimacy of these private companies, but it will insist that the trend toward privatising military functions should not open the door to a weakening of respect for IHL and for its implementation."[92] Thus, the search for security in the contemporary marketplace has led even august aid agencies like the ICRC to move beyond denouncing the private option and develop formal procedures for subcontracting for security services.

From the perspective of societies themselves, another consideration is whether the application of military force from intervening governments does more harm than good, which requires applying the problematic calculations of consequentialist ethics. What was formerly a field of human endeavor dominated by duty-based (deontological) ethics – humanitarian acts are simply good in and of themselves no matter what the consequences – has shifted toward a consideration of outcomes. Instead of the moral absolutes that many humanitarians espouse as part of their worldview, situational ethics are now required, what the late pioneer of forced migration studies Myron Wiener called "instrumental humanitarianism."[93] The devil lies in the details, as folk wisdom would have it. The question is: where does the balance lie, if we weigh the positive against the negative effects? The real difficulty lies in determining whether using the military will help bring about a better outcome than the available alternatives. The various controversies in determining the least-bad result include: weighing the consequences for whom; whether we should think in terms of the results from individual acts or rules to govern general domains of actions; the appropriate time horizon for evaluating consequences; and the uncertainty that surrounds any action and its possible impacts. Hugo Slim refers to an apt cooking metaphor in reminding us why pragmatic mixtures are required for decision-making: "Like oil and vinegar, ideals and reality never fully dissolve into one another and tend naturally to separate if left alone. To combine, they need to be regularly stirred up together if they are to make a good vinaigrette."[94]

There is now a widespread recognition that humanitarian relief will almost always have some negative and unintended consequences – David Kennedy's "dark sides of virtue"[95] – and that the use of the military entails complications for any calculation of benefits and costs. As it is impossible to know all of the effects of aid or of military force, the issue therefore is whether, on balance, they cause more good than harm.[96] Accordingly, many humanitarian agencies refer to consequentialism as they evaluate their efforts. The overwhelmingly and generally agreed negative outcomes in Rwanda and Bosnia started the soul-searching, along with donors' desire for evidence of effectiveness and impact. How can such acts be considered ethical if acting on the moral obligation to help those in need leads to feeding those killers mingling with victimized populations in refugee camps or prolonging war by offering a portion of food aid to combatants in exchange for access to victims?

There are also significant quantitative problems regarding the actual measurement of costs and benefits. Establishing a bottom line for the benefits to civilians in a targeted country resulting from coercive intervention by external military forces requires determining and assessing the economic costs of the military intervention itself along with the casualties, fatalities, and political impact of such an outside intervention. Determining the civilian benefits of intervention in a targeted country requires assessing accurately the difference before and after an intervention in terms of such factors as displacement (numbers of refugees, IDPs, and besieged populations), suffering (hunger, disease, and human rights abuse), and the state of the local polity (its ability to exercise sovereignty).

Any reader who has tried to attach values to social scientific questions should immediately realize the challenge of such an exercise. The lack of longitudinal data – or a common understanding of what number-crunchers would call "stylized facts" – sometimes poses close to insurmountable problems.[97] Armed forces are not forthcoming about data, nor do they employ comparable accounting methods. Humanitarian agencies are hardly better, each using its own form of accounting that makes comparisons across agencies impossible. Moreover, reliable statistics about the actual costs of delivering goods and alternatives are sketchy and not comparable among sources or sectors.

Furthermore, an enormous source of ambiguity arises in attaching a value to human life itself. Such stalwart defenders of humanitarian action as Ian Smillie and Larry Minear acknowledge just how painful making ethical decisions has become: "In recent years, the moral necessity of humanitarian action is no longer self-evident and has become a matter of debate."[98] "'Moral calculus' is not a highly developed form of mathematics," note Marc Lindenberg and Coralie Bryant. "It is hard to know whether one hundred lives saved is worth the price of having inadvertently helped to prolong a conflict by a month. It is even hard to document the numbers of lives lost and saved in such situations."[99]

How can analysts measure impacts within affected areas without assigning a specific monetary value to a human being? For some critics, each and every life has an infinite value; and if so, cost–benefit analyses are beside the point. But for most analysts it will be necessary to assign a concrete value, and thus they must be willing to wander in this philosophical and moral minefield.

In an effort to assess the pluses and minuses of humanitarian intervention in the 1990s, I used the image of Olympic diving as part of any judgment because an evaluator needs to consider the degrees of difficulty and of execution to fairly evaluate the overall utility of a particular military intervention.[100] Factors entering into the judgment include: the danger and chaos of a particular humanitarian situation; the physical challenge of a specific terrain; and the ambitiousness of a concrete mandate.

Taking into account the above considerations, my own judgment is that northern Iraq in 1991, Haiti, East Timor, and Kosovo are at one end of the spectrum with the benefits to civilians (in terms of lives saved, improved access, and fewer rights violations) worth the economic, military, and political costs. At the other end would be pre-Dayton Bosnia because the high economic and political costs and low effectiveness of the military forces were not commensurate with the civilian benefits. Indeed, the half-hearted military intervention there perpetuated violence in some areas such as the "safe zones," where the concentration of Bosnian Muslims facilitated mass slaughter. The most notable example is Srebrenica – one of the so-called safe zones under the protection of UN troops – where Serbian forces systematically killed over 8,000 Bosnian Muslim men and boys.

In between, I would place Rwanda closer to the successful end of the spectrum, especially after July 1994 – ironically because the military expenditures were non-existent earlier and rather trivial over a concentrated period of a few months. Most of the bloodshed had already unfolded as powerful states stood by. Thus, while the benefits to civilians resulting from the eventual intervention in terms of humanitarian assistance and eventual repatriation were considerable, overall the international community of states failed to halt or abate one of the worst genocides of the post-World War II period.

Somalia would be closer to the failure end, especially because of the subsequent backlash against multilateralism in the United States, thereby leading to Washington's refusal to label the massive bloodshed in Rwanda "genocide" and thus to act. Of course, Rwanda or Somalia – or any of the other cases, for that matter – could be pushed closer to either end of the spectrum by a shift in subjective appreciation or an emphasis (or de-emphasis) on particular data or priorities or weighting of variables. Omniscience is not usually a skill available to military and humanitarian planners.

The final outcomes of the 2011 interventions in Libya with NATO air power and in Côte d'Ivoire with UN forces, especially the French contingent, are unknown as of this writing. The ousting of Gaddafi and the installation of President Outarra in Abidjan are heartening and perhaps harbingers. In mid-2012, Libya held its first democratic elections with the moderate Nationalist Forces Alliance victorious over Islamist rivals, a relief to NATO powers. However, violent militias and corruption still plague the country. Meanwhile in Côte d'Ivoire, intermittent violence continued to prompt displacement, while the June 2012 attack on UN peacekeepers which led to the deaths of 16 individuals, including 8 civilians, has exacerbated security concerns. As we have seen, uncertainty is the only certainty in our measurements, which makes many dedicated humanitarians truly uneasy. However, politics – including double standards and inconsistencies – are a fact of humanitarian or any other life.

Whatever the morality and law affecting humanitarian space and the humanitarian marketplace, political will and military capacity ultimately are more important in determining when, where, why, and how to protect and assist vulnerable populations.[101] The 2011 international action in Libya was unusual in that moral, legal, political, and military dimensions coincided under the R2P rubric.[102] However shocking to the conscience a particular emergency and however hard or soft the applicable public international law, when political will and a military capacity exist, humanitarian space will open in which war victims will receive relief and protection. The addition of the moral and legal dimensions in Libya was significant.

One final consideration about the use of military force for human protection purposes comes from a different type of naysayer who worries about the potential blowback from moral hazard. In economic theory, moral hazard arises when a party insulated from risk by insurance behaves differently from how it would otherwise if it were fully exposed to the consequences of risk.

Alan Kuperman is one of a growing band of contrarians who argues that the expectation of benefiting from possible outside intervention – and he includes sanctions, embargoes, judicial pursuit, and military force – emboldens sub-state groups of rebels either to launch or continue fighting in order, among other things, to benefit from war and aid economies.[103] The evidence is largely anecdotal, but undoubtedly international involvement has affected the calculations of local militias and elites, even causing them to take action that perhaps had the effect, intended and unintended, of prolonging violence.

But does this mean that robust humanitarianism is inevitably destined to constitute a moral hazard? The theory applies to specific circumstances. Clearly people who purchase automobile insurance do not usually drive more recklessly any more than those who purchase health or home insurance ignore their physical well-being or build bonfires in their living rooms.

Perhaps there would be a problem if humanitarians had the sort of insurance policy that allows banks to be reckless with other people's money. However, there is no such global life insurance policy, and combatants and vulnerable populations know this. The opposite problem is more likely: everyone knows that talk is cheap.[104] If the International Criminal Court's issuing an arrest warrant for Sudanese president Omar al-Bashir is as empty a threat as the use of outside military force to halt the slow-motion genocide in Darfur, then it is not so much moral hazard that is the problem but rather collective spinelessness. The moral hazard argument, if taken literally, could lead to the conclusion that pledging to do nothing is the right thing, which would certainly have human consequences and potentially grant perpetrators a blank check. The conclusion that outsiders should evaluate the range of possible impacts of their assistance, however, is crystal clear, and in that sense moral hazard is a valuable consideration for those in the marketplace who wish to avoid perverse incentives.

Conclusion

Wars and the humanitarianism business have changed over the past few decades. Not everything is new under the sun; but in many arenas, there is certainly novelty. The horrors of so-called old or new wars (death, injury, displacement) and the demands placed on aid agencies (for resources) are constants, but the conditions under which humanitarians operate have changed and thus sharply altered the meaning of the professional activities that concern us here.

A dramatic expansion in the humanitarian marketplace has been visible, as has the burgeoning range of activities associated with humanitarianism. This growth, in resources and ambitions, is viewed by some as a step in the right direction and by others as quite the opposite. Michael Ignatieff and David Rieff, for example, evaluate recent trends as the construction of a "humanitarian empire" or "humanitarian recolonization," respectively.[105]

In tandem with the growing number of crises, agencies, resources, and types of actors, humanitarian agencies themselves have also taken decisions to expand: organizations that were once dedicated to relief have expanded into other domains; and organizations that had a dual mandate (i.e., relief and development) but never really considered the relationship between relief and non-relief goals have been obliged to do so. That is, agencies of various types are moving both "upstream" (toward helping in the midst of war) and "downstream" (toward post-conflict peacebuilding and ultimately development). Few UN organizations or international NGOs do not carry the mantle of broad-brush humanitarianism as an essential part of their identities and work plans.

"Towards the end of the 1990s, a new or political humanitarianism emerged, claiming to correct the wrongs of the past," is how Mark Duffield summarized the current state of play. "Rather than humanitarian assistance as a universal right and as a good thing in itself, the new humanitarianism is based on a consequentialist framework."[106] Duffield is critical of this development; I am not. This chapter suggests the extent to which humility is a prerequisite for aid workers and researchers treading on the contemporary landscape of new wars and new humanitarianisms.

It is now appropriate to journey more deeply into the unregulated business arena where humanitarians operate. What is the role of coordination and competition?

CHAPTER THREE

Coordination vs. Competition in an Unregulated Market

The focus of this chapter is on the various and sundry moving parts of the international humanitarian system. Indeed, "system" is a misnomer unless the adjective "feudal" accompanies it. Every organization within the business ferociously guards its independence. In fact, a cartoonist could not have come up with a better design for futile complexity than the current array of UN organizations and international NGOs. On the UN side, we see agencies focusing on a substantive area whose headquarters are often located in a different country or continent from other relevant partners and with separate budgets, governing boards, and organizational cultures as well as independent executive heads. On the NGO side, the numbers are even greater and the decentralization as well, with even the partners in a common federation having differing views depending on their country affiliation.

The potential contribution as well as potential confusion resulting from the bevy of actors that flocks to the scene of a human-made disaster should have emerged from the previous two chapters. Here, we discuss the nature of coordination, the purported solution for some of the problems in the humanitarian business, as well as the history of both UN and NGO coordinating efforts, before concluding with the dominant competition for resources that is a predictable downside of a completely unregulated marketplace.

What Coordination and Why?

Readers may wonder why I sometimes use scare quotes around common expressions. It is because they surround words that obfuscate more than clarify. Hence, calls for enhanced "coordination" are usually sung by a passionate chorus of bureaucrats whose actual behavior reflects administrative inertia and the dominant economic incentives pushing in the direction of going-it-alone. The widespread shorthand to describe the totality of actors is usually the international humanitarian "system." This word disguises the fact that overall performance reflects the sum of individual actions rather than a planned and coherent whole. Other images, the international humanitarian "family" or "clan," are more apt in allowing for the fact that, like many such units, the humanitarian versions are extremely dysfunctional.

The need to make better use of the many moving parts of international institutions seemingly has been a preoccupation of donors, aid practitioners, and analysts for quite some time. It arises with great fanfare every time a major disaster strikes – Biafra, East Pakistan, Ethiopia, northern Iraq, Somalia, Rwanda, Haiti, and the list goes on. High-intensity pressure for change is registered only while agencies have mud on their faces because of clumsy delivery and publicized mistakes. But just as quickly, the pressure for change evaporates. Meanwhile, the actors go back to business-as-usual, and the striking inefficiency of the system continues. The crying need to have less waste and more impact at least within the international delivery system seems especially compelling when huge numbers of lives are at stake in humanitarian catastrophes. "For some of the UN system clan members, the word 'coordination' tends to summon up visions of ignorant meddlers pushing microphones and cameras into their realms," notes long-time UN observer Leon Gordenker. "For others, it means combining talents to achieve better results. It may also offer a channel by which some help can be made available for UN peace-maintaining tasks. Perhaps for all it signifies yet more meetings and documents. For none does it mean hierarchical commands from somewhere on high."[1]

Everyone is for coordination as long as – surprise, surprise – it implies no loss of autonomy or decision-making authority. One retired UN practitioner with a wide variety of country experiences, Antonio Donini, draws distinctions among three broad categories of coordination within the United Nations, but they apply equally to the rest of the humanitarian business: *coordination by command* – in other words, coordination where strong leadership is accompanied by some sort of leverage and authority, whether carrot or stick; *coordination by consensus* – where leadership is essentially a function of the capacity of the "coordinator" to orchestrate a coherent response and to mobilize the key actors around common objectives and priorities; and *coordination by default* – where, in the absence of a formal coordination entity, only the most rudimentary exchange of information and division of labor takes place among the actors.[2]

The feudal nature of the UN system and the ferocious independence of international NGOs are accompanied by the desire from donor governments – and especially recalcitrant members of the parliaments that approve budgets and want to keep constituents satisfied – to wave their own national flags and receive appropriate credit for any donations. However desirable, coordination by command is unrealistic. While exceptions occur – for instance, some have argued that the UNHCR exercised "benign coercive coordination" as lead agency in the Balkans in the early 1990s – the experience under the best of circumstances could undoubtedly be most accurately described as coordination by consensus. A subjective agreement to work together emerges from the personalities of the personnel on the ground; but there is no structural explanation while the incentive structure is ignored. The experience under the worst of circumstances – for instance, in the uncharted waters of Liberia or Afghanistan or Iraq – demonstrated the total absence of meaningful coordination; and what little existed could accurately be labeled as coordination by default. Other options were even worse.

Can we not do better? The central theme in the earlier discussion of contemporary war zones and humanitarian identity crises is the urgent requirement for fewer outsiders with far better orchestration and more professionalism among those coming to the rescue – the military, IGOs and especially the members of the UN system, international NGOs, private contractors, and the ICRC.

"Coordination," a Fool's Errand?

As one might surmise from the brief comments to date, no expression in the international public policy lexicon is more used, and less in evidence, than "coordination." Autonomy, not meaningful coordination, is the key goal of proprietary UN agencies and market-share-oriented NGOs; these are familiar collective action problems inherent in today's marketplace in spite of previous experiments to counter such forces within the UN and NGO universes.

The UN System

Intergovernmental organizations are prominent in the humanitarian marketplace, and logically one might expect the United Nations to take the lead in making the most not only of its own organizations but also of orchestrating inputs from other humanitarian partners. Who is better placed than the senior staff of the universal membership world organization?

This seemingly logical question, however, does not have a simple answer. The relative simplicity that the reader found in Figure 1.1 fails to capture the numbers of actors and contrasting agendas and priorities that appear within each cell of what appear as pristine categories. Why?

First, the problem of what counts as UN humanitarianism is not as obvious as it appears. The main UN humanitarian players in terms of resources and expertise are the UNHCR for refugees, UNICEF for women and children, and the WFP for food and logistics. While these units were born as humanitarians, other UN bodies were created decades ago to foster development but are increasingly involved in relief and reconstruction because of growing available resources, including the UNDP and the World Bank, both of which have moved steadily upstream toward the eye of the humanitarian storm rather than pursuing their comparative advantage as development specialists. Similarly, UN specialized agencies – for example, the World Health Organization and the UN Educational, Scientific and Cultural Organization – once had virtually non-existent disaster programs but have expanded to meet the new demand and availability of funding. Consequently, UN institutions that might not have counted as humanitarian in the 1980s today have at least modest and sometimes quite substantial operations.

Second, previous efforts have excluded consolidation or centralization; most importantly, budgetary authority remains within each organization. The establishment of OCHA (which we learned earlier was preceded by the DHA and by UNDRO) was an empty administrative gesture. In December 1991, on the heels of the clumsy efforts by humanitarian suppliers in the Persian Gulf War, General Assembly resolution 46/182 called for an emergency relief coordinator to harmonize diplomacy and implementing UN humanitarian efforts. In April 1992, then newly elected secretary-general Boutros

Boutros-Ghali allocated an under-secretary-general post to the new Department of Humanitarian Affairs and appointed Jan Eliasson, the able Swedish ambassador in New York who had helped to negotiate the end to the Iran–Iraq War in 1987 and to shepherd the controversial resolution 46/182 through the General Assembly.[3]

As a national from a progressive donor country at the head of a department established in response to donor dissatisfactions, Eliasson pursued four tasks seen as crucial by donor governments: gather and manage information; define, prioritize, and consolidate requirements for donors; negotiate interagency frameworks for action and orchestrate field activities; and provide low-key leadership.[4]

Behind the public eloquence, however, basic management ineptitude was hiding along with the absence of any leverage over resources. The DHA and then OCHA after 1998 have made too little practical difference during their existence under Eliasson, as well as his successors: Peter Hansen, a respected Danish development economist with lengthy UN experience; Yasushi Akashi, who had held a number of senior UN posts in New York and in peace operations in Cambodia and the former Yugoslavia; Sergio Vieira de Mello, a "UN-lifer" who led operations in the Balkans and East Timor before becoming the UN high commissioner for human rights and then the special representative in Iraq until he was killed there in August 2003; Kenzo Oshima, who held several senior-level positions in the Japanese government related to humanitarian assistance and development; Jan Egeland, who was secretary-general of the Norwegian Red Cross and has had active experience in humanitarian, human rights, and peace work through the UN, the Norwegian government, and the Red Cross and Red Crescent movement before heading the Norwegian Institute of International Affairs and Human Rights Watch Europe; and then two British nationals, John

Holmes, a career diplomat, and subsequently Valerie Amos, a former minister with substantial experience in addressing poverty in Africa as well as the promotion of human rights, social justice, and equality on that continent.

Intriguingly, an effort to pull together the various moving parts of the international humanitarian system almost took place in 1997; and it is worth exploring that case to understand why something so sensible as consolidation is seemingly so impossible. After all, the decentralization of the UN's humanitarian capabilities does not only result in the well-documented competition within the UN system, the difficulties in dealing with IDPs, and the often ineffective linkages between UN military and humanitarian operations, but it also hampers assistance to and protection of civilians menaced by mass atrocities.

A long-standing yet orphaned proposal, namely to create a consolidated UN agency to assist and protect war victims, seemed sensible after the problems of the early post-Cold War era. This amalgamation was to entail the UNHCR, the WFP, UNICEF, and the UNDP along with what was to become the UN Secretariat's OCHA. Such a consolidation would have had the advantage not only of addressing squarely the problems of assisting and protecting refugees and others in "refugee-like situations" (mainly IDPs, who have no legal or institutional home) but also of attenuating the legendary waste and turf battles among UN organizations. It would have involved the consolidation of parts of the United Nations organization proper and thus not required constitutional changes. Eventually, it could have embraced major international NGOs as part of a collective effort, but that was really a bridge too far.

In fact, the unthinkable reform almost came about when Secretary-General Kofi Annan ordered a system-wide review of the world organization with especial attention to humanitarian operations at the outset of his first mandate in 1997.[5]

The penultimate draft of a report by Maurice Strong, the Canadian businessman with significant UN experience during the previous quarter-century, proposed a merging of UN emergency activities but even more importantly had an appendix that fleshed out the longer-term possibility of creating a consolidated UN humanitarian agency.

Other UN agencies – especially UNICEF and the WFP – as well as NGOs through their US consortium InterAction saw a threat to their existence: the UNHCR would loom over them in size and authority, and their budgets and personnel would dwindle and someday be subsumed in a new consolidated agency. Annan backed off in light of the fierce opposition led by the very same donors who preached coherence and consolidation but had their own agendas as well – including protecting the territory and budget allocations of their favorite IGOs and NGOs in quintessential patron–client relationships. The final version of the 1997 reorganization hatched a mouse: a repackaging of the former Department of Humanitarian Affairs as OCHA.

The old-wine-in-a-new-bottle routine was not lost on the final group of eminent persons organized during the Kofi Annan era, the High-level Panel on UN System-wide Coherence on Development, Humanitarian Assistance and the Environment. Its recommendations for consolidation, or "delivering as one," have largely met the same inglorious fate as earlier calls, including Robert Jackson's classic and oft-cited 1969 *Capacity Study*.[6] Pulling together the various moving parts of the UN's humanitarian machinery represents a lofty aspiration, not a feasible policy recommendation.

NGO Coordination Part 1: Federations

While national chapters of NGOs remain autonomous, many of the largest and most visible organizations have over the past several decades formed partnerships with similar brethren in other countries. While it would be a stretch to describe this as "centralization," it does qualify as loose "coordination" across borders. It would be useful to describe in detail four of the most significant federations.

The Oxford Committee for Famine Relief was founded in England in 1944 to raise funds to provide food for civilians in Nazi-occupied Greece during World War II. Later renamed "Oxfam" after its shortened and more familiar acronym (we saw the same branding for UNICEF above and will also see it for CARE below) and currently headquartered in London, it is a confederation of 15 national affiliates, two observer members, and a secretariat for the group called Oxfam International. Oxfam also maintains six advocacy and campaigning offices.

Until recently, the Oxfam International board was comprised of voting and non-voting trustees from each national affiliate, consisting of the chairs of the boards and of the executive directors for each affiliate, respectively. However, in 2011 the governance structure was changed so that each affiliate sits on the Oxfam International board as a member (with one vote each), with the right to nominate individuals to attend meetings. In the last few years, Oxfam International has attempted to generate a more coherent collective brand identity for all affiliates. This includes implementation of a "Single Management Structure" project, which reflects in part an internal perception of inadequate coordination of media communications, an increasingly important element in fundraising and advocacy.

The total program expenditure by Oxfam affiliates in the 2009–10 fiscal year was almost $850 million,[7] and Oxfam International's secretariat had revenue of some $5.6 million. Virtually all of that revenue came from affiliates' dues, with only 2 percent generated from donations, legacies, and goods in kind. About 20 percent of the secretariat's budget was devoted to "confederation development," which consists of activities to support the growth of affiliates, and to increase overall revenue, including financial support for prospective affiliates, and inter-affiliate activities to promote revenue growth for particular members. Oxfam also supports newer and smaller affiliates with start-up grants and loans, which accounted for about 35 percent of the expenditures in a typical financial year.[8]

CARE was founded in 1945 as the Cooperative for American Remittances to Europe in order to provide food relief for those starving on the continent in the wake of World War II. Eventually millions of "CARE packages" were sent to people in Europe, and later to various areas of the developing world. The object itself was so successful that it entered into the colloquial language: for instance, parents sometimes send "CARE packages" to their children at camp or university. A geographical expansion of CARE's mission led to a name change to Cooperative for Assistance and Relief Everywhere, but eventually the acronym alone was used, CARE International. The organization has grown in size and the breadth of its mission to become a leading international humanitarian organization, focused on combating global poverty, and especially on the plight of women as a key strategy in this mission. In 2010 CARE operated in 87 countries, on poverty reduction programs, disaster relief, and advocacy, with a staff of around 12,000.

CARE International is a federation of 12 national members, with a secretariat in Geneva. The organization also maintains liaison offices in Brussels and New York. The affiliates are autonomous, conducting project decision-making at the national level, while the secretariat provides coordination and support for its members' activities, as well as advocacy, and representation at the United Nations and European Union. Members agree to abide by a CARE International code of conduct, and the secretariat tries to ensure compliance. CARE International's board oversees activities and usually meets twice a year; with a chair (elected by the board) and two members from each affiliate: the national director and a local board representative.

CARE International raised $795 million in 2010, ranging from $6 million, or 0.75 percent, for the Thai affiliate, to $586 million, or 74 percent, for the US one. Most affiliates receive the majority of their revenue from government and NGO grants and donor contributions (over 50 percent from grants alone for most affiliates). In 2010 CARE spent $805 million, of which 81 percent went toward program work.[9]

Médecins sans Frontières, or Doctors without Borders, was founded in 1971 by two groups of physicians working in disaster relief. One group had worked for the ICRC during the Biafra civil war in Nigeria in the late 1960s, and the other in eastern Pakistan in 1970, helping the victims of a tsunami. Staff in both crises had become disillusioned with the principles (especially neutrality and impartiality) and practices (especially discretion) of existing humanitarian organizations and the ICRC in particular. Taking sides and speaking out (*témoinage*, or witnessing) on behalf of victims became their commitment.

MSF is a major humanitarian NGO federation whose active field members are largely doctors and other healthcare workers. Structurally, the organization consists of 19 national offices and MSF International, whose secretariat is based in Geneva. The latter coordinates policy and activities between the national offices, and attempts to maintain standards of accountability and transparency. MSF also has 10 "satellite" organizations, each specialized in a certain area such as relief supplies or medical research, and which operate independently of headquarters.

MSF's total expenditure in 2010 was about $1.1 billion with

a surplus of some $176 million.[10] Of this revenue, almost 91 percent came from the national offices with donations by individuals and private institutions (primarily corporations, trusts, and foundations). In keeping with the organization's attempt to maintain independence from governments, less than 10 percent of total income came from government treasuries (Canada, Denmark, Germany, Ireland, Spain, Switzerland, and ECHO).

National affiliates have budgets ranging from $6.9 million for Greece to almost $270 million for the United States. About 50 percent of MSF's expenditure in 2010 went toward field staff costs, with a further 20 percent going toward medical purchases (including drugs, equipment, and hospitalization). By region, 58 percent of expenditure was for Africa, with a further 21 percent and 18 percent on the Americas and Asia, respectively. Owing to the January 2010 earthquake in Haiti, and the proximity of the United States (the largest MSF donor), the organization spent almost $140 million there on disaster relief that year, almost double that spent on the next highest receiver of aid, the DRC.

Save the Children was founded in England in 1919 to help children malnourished and otherwise in ill health in central Europe in the aftermath of World War I. The organization started in response to the British blockade of Germany and Austria, which had contributed to the dire suffering of these children. The organization provides relief aid and promotes children's rights in 120 countries. The umbrella Save the Children Association consists of 29 national organizations, and a coordinating and support office in London, Save the Children International, which is a wholly owned subsidiary of the association. The organization also has advocacy offices in Addis Ababa, Brussels, Geneva, and New York. The organization is governed by the board of Save the Children International.

In 2010 the organization's total income was $1.4 billion, ranging from some $300,000 raised by the Jordanian organization to almost $550 million by the US affiliate – between them, the US and UK branches accounted for about 65 percent of all revenue in 2010.[11] In the last few years the organization has begun moving toward the goal of unity as a single global movement. For example, in 2010 the association developed financial and quality controls to improve efficiency in information sharing and accountability. The national organizations have also all agreed to a joint mission and strategy.

World Vision was founded in the 1950s by an American war correspondent and evangelist to help children orphaned during the Korean War. The organization today is a major US-based evangelical Christian NGO that is involved in disaster relief, community development, and advocacy in almost 100 countries. World Vision International is the coordinating body for the local affiliates (the World Vision Partnership), providing oversight of operations and representing the organization globally through offices in 10 cities worldwide.

While the affiliates are governed by their own boards, there is a Covenant of Partnership that binds affiliates to common standards and policies. Much decision-making is local, however, with over 90 percent of projects approved at the affiliate level. The affiliates also endeavor to hold one other accountable via a peer-review procedure. World Vision International had income of just over $1 billion in 2010; about 75 percent came from private sources, and the rest from the US government, with approximately 85 percent devoted to programs.[12]

What is apparent from the above examples is that coordination is loose, at best, even within organizations sharing a common acronym and program objectives. While federations are international, local affiliates are influenced by the countries where they are based and where fundraising takes place. The resources devoted to developing mechanisms to improve coherence across borders, moreover, are relatively small in comparison to total outlays, suggesting the low priority attached to it. The similarities with the UN system should be obvious because there exists no hierarchy of control; whatever coordination takes place is a function of good will and personalities not structure or financial incentives.

NGO Coordination Part 2: Consortia

Efforts to pull together affiliates in federations across national boundaries have been echoed by attempts to form consortia across borders (of institutions and countries). It is worth illustrating by discussing efforts by NGOs in the United States and Europe: InterAction in Washington, DC, the International Council for Voluntary Action (ICVA) in Geneva, and Voluntary Organizations Cooperating in Emergencies (VOICE) in Brussels.

The American Council for Voluntary International Action, more commonly known as InterAction, is the largest United States-based consortium of international NGOs. It has more than 200 members, which collectively seek to coordinate work in developing countries in which members operate. The consortium coordinates attempts to have an impact on US government policy on a range of development and humanitarian issues, provides information to members on the location and nature of the project locations of other members, and conducts media advocacy and outreach.

InterAction's members agree to follow standards of accountability and transparency in relation to finance, governance, and program implementation. Its strategy for the 2011–14 period identifies as priority tasks: a unified lobbying stance with the US government; raising the public profile of its members; and aiding members in generating partnerships with governments, UN agencies, local civil society actors, and the private sector. The total annual revenue of InterAction's members is estimated to be $13 billion. The consortium's own income in 2010 was a measly $5.7 million, with about half coming from member dues.[13] The allocation of some .04 percent to common activities suggests the low importance attached to the common cause.

The Geneva-based International Council of Voluntary Agencies is a global consortium of over 70 humanitarian NGOs that attempts to shape international policymaking on issues affecting its members, provides them with information on developments in humanitarian policy areas, and provides some field support. ICVA members meet in a General Assembly, which is the broad agenda setter, responsible for creating and overseeing the organization's policies. The assembly aims to meet every three years, and elects the consortium's Executive Committee, which meets at least every six months to provide more detailed direction for the organization. The policies of these two bodies are implemented by the organization's secretariat. The costs of running the secretariat in 2010 were about $1 million, with about 35 percent coming from member dues and most of the rest from grants from government (e.g., Denmark, the Netherlands, Norway, and Switzerland) that presumably are investing in more coordination for NGOs.

Voluntary Organizations in Cooperation in Emergencies is a network consisting of 83 European humanitarian NGOs, whose primary goal is to influence EU and member state policymaking. Members include British and Irish Christian Aid, the Norwegian Refugee Council, and German development and emergency relief NGO Welthungerhilfe. It also includes the affiliates of various NGO federations, including CARE Austria, Save the Children Denmark, Oxfam GB, and World Vision Finland. VOICE is the most significant nongovernmental liaison organization with the EU on humanitarian issues – lobbying for its members' policy and especially funding priorities with the European Commission, the Council of the EU, and the European Parliament. VOICE makes administrative and organizational decisions through its General Assembly, which gathers the member organizations annually. The assembly also elects the chair of the board of directors, the VOICE president, for three years and establishes advocacy priorities.

VOICE's revenue for 2010 was around $570,000, of which 70 percent came from membership fees.[14] The organization also receives a grant from ECHO. Most VOICE members have also signed up to ECHO's Framework Partnership Agreement, receiving grants in return for following the commission's procedures in relation to humanitarian assistance, which include bilateral exchanges of information and highlighting the EU role in their humanitarian projects.

As with the UN system and NGO federations, only the loosest and vaguest coordination is the best that can be hoped for with consortia. Information is shared and guidelines are developed, but no authority can be exerted over such voluntary associations. And the results have been comparable: occasional success based on individuals and their commitments but not on any coherent structure or organizational chart that would guarantee a more business-like performance on a regular basis.

Competition and Turf

We return to the lament heard from numerous NGO and UN officials: "Everyone is for coordination but nobody wants to be coordinated." Will it ever be possible to consolidate the various moving parts of the humanitarian system? Why is there so much competition over turf? Earlier we discussed the growth in numbers and in overall resources in relationship to the nature of the business. Part of the reason for the increase in resources flows from the global neoliberal tide. In trimming down bureaucracies in accordance with free-market imperatives, states now dole out contracts to NGOs for tasks once undertaken by public agencies, but they have not abandoned control over how those resources are used or where. Based on data collected by Michael Barnett and Rebecca Cohen on funding sources, Fearon's analysis of the humanitarian industry revealed a tripling in the total number of NGOs funded by USAID from 1982 to 2003.[15]

NGO staffs have increased dramatically in tandem with the market shares of the largest agencies. Between 1997 and 2005, the numbers of people working in the NGO sector grew by 91 percent while overall the international humanitarian system (if the UN system and the ICRC are also included) experienced a 77 percent surge in personnel.[16] Dramatic crises also generate spikes for specific emergencies, which tend to increase the base for longer-run development as well. For instance, over 200 international NGOs were reported on the ground in the first weeks of operations in Sarajevo and Kigali in 1992 and 1993, respectively.

It should be noted, however, that these totals undoubtedly underestimate the growth because we can only easily count those organizations based in the West. While resources and institutions mainly come from industrialized countries, an active but largely unknown relief sector exists in the non-Western world, especially in Islamic countries. This underreported reality is especially pertinent since about half of war victims since the 1990s are Muslim. Hence, it is unfortunate that speculation and uninformed accounts have trumped the search for knowledge and insights since September 11; rather than research about humanitarian efforts, most attention is directed at the putative connections between Islamic charitable organizations and terrorism,[17] and more especially diasporas.[18]

Here we examine the incentives driving the competition for resources and visibility in this increasingly crowded business. Figure 3.1 is an important point of departure for this discussion and should be consulted and understood alongside Figure 1.1 (external and internal actors that affect the humanitarian response in a particular war zone). The illustration here attempts to capture the international flow of resources to the various organizations actively delivering assistance or protecting affected populations. Either as taxpayers or as individual contributors to charitable organizations, readers should be able to trace how their public or private dollar or euro or pound helps finance humanitarian operations.

Indeed, the figure suggests what might well be seen as a "spaghetti junction" of influence, reflecting the numerous origins of resources flowing to various actors. The multiple arrows suggest the most rampant material factors driving aid agency behavior: namely, the institutional rivalries grounded in a struggle for funding and market share. Like all ventures and all organizations, those in the humanitarian marketplace require resources to carry out desirable activities in a particular area of operations as well as to pay salaries, rents, equipment, transportation, and overheads. Survival is a minimum goal; prosperity is the real objective. As MSF's Fabrice Weissman straightforwardly tells us: "[A]id agencies [are] ever sensitive to the preservation and growth of their budgets."[19]

Humanitarianism raises a host of issues that characterize any business, ranging from the mechanics of branding and retailing to the consequences of competition. Alexander Cooley and James Ron have used the image of "the NGO scramble," but all intergovernmental and private institutions (nonprofits as well as for-profit private contractors) face comparable pressures and imperatives if they are to survive and thrive in the humanitarian marketplace.

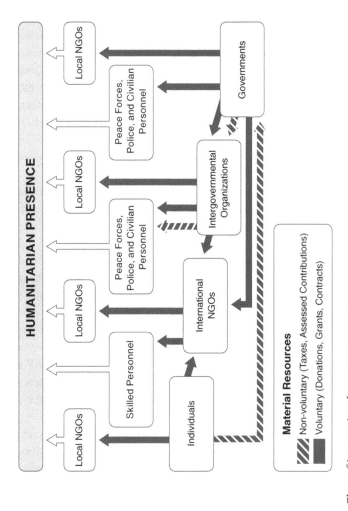

Figure 3.1 Flow of international resources to a war zone

What seems "normal" business sense and practice for farmers and steel companies, however, seems unbecoming and even morally reprehensible for aid agencies attempting to save lives in war zones. Nonetheless, aid agencies are obliged to pursue fundraising, which means, as Cooley and Ron note, that "dysfunctional organizational behavior is likely to be a rational response to systematic and predictable institutional pressures."[20] To point to material incentives and rent-seeking is not to criticize individuals or impugn their moral values but rather to demonstrate the power of the market for the humanitarian business in addition to the power of the humanitarian ethos.

The availability of material resources can influence the decision to participate in or defect from a joint effort; and what comes to mind in this context is Mancur Olson's classic work explaining the logic to "free ride" on the efforts of others rather than participate in collective action. Mustering sufficient resources to fund programs is, of course, essential to any enterprise; but the tunnel vision of individual agencies often blinds decision-makers to the collective dimensions of their work. Although Olson's case studies relate to cooperation among states, a similar logic applies to humanitarian organizations. He demonstrates that a variety of units sharing common goals often end up operating in ways that undermine presumed intentions.[21] As such, negative results do not reflect bad faith but rather ingrained, improper incentives as well as poor knowledge about the system's functions. Humanitarian organizations often publicly espouse altruistic objectives but essentially pursue more self-centered ones not only to address the emergency needs of distressed populations but also to thrive as institutions in a competitive marketplace. As Alex de Waal finds, business units have two sets of interests: "soft" (relief and protection) and "hard" (organizational survival and growth),[22] which may clash.

This unregulated, increasingly crowded market generates strong incentives for privileging "hard" interests, sometimes at the expense of "soft" ones. This section highlights the consequences of an increasingly competitive marketplace for the collective humanitarian endeavor. First, within a war zone itself, the existence of multiple possible contractors increases the ability of spoilers and potential spoilers to play contractors and donors off against one another. For example, if an aid agency purchases access to victims through bribes – often in the form of a "tax" on goods transported to affected populations – this behavior may not only have an impact on war victims but may also establish a precedent whereby all agencies are expected to buy access in the same way – or perhaps even bid up the price. Some exploitative interlocutors may be "shopping" for agencies that can give them the best deal (i.e., allow for the greatest extortion).

For example, in Sierra Leone, agencies were played off against one another by the warring parties.[23] The Security Council went so far as to castigate aid organizations for deviating from a coherent framework for engagement. It later concluded from the experience that "common ground rules would help to make access negotiations more predictable and effective" and reduce the risk of manipulation by belligerents. Unfortunately, the problem was not lack of ground rules but the availability of alternative sources of supply from agencies whose "hard" interests were better served by ignoring them.

In less bureaucratic language, individual agencies that cut their own deals with those who are gatekeepers to victims essentially up the ante for other agencies. For individual organizations, the fear of being marginalized from humanitarian crises can drive them to join in pursuing a collective effort that they abhor. Why? Withdrawal may lower the media profile of defectors, which can in turn hurt not only fundraising and programming for other activities in a particular war zone, but also efforts to mobilize resources for projects in other parts of the world. Oftentimes an individual agency's reputation, profile, and fundraising leverage result from being present in the toughest of circumstances. What is rational and productive for one agency may be quite irrational and counterproductive for the humanitarian enterprise as a whole.

Second, funders are prime movers in the humanitarian business, and as agencies face more and more competitors for grants and contracts, donors acquire greater leverage to affect decision-making by individual organizations at every level. Donor preferences structure how operational agencies cast their programs to qualify for as large a share of the humanitarian pie as possible. The expansion by humanitarians into post-conflict (or development) activities and by development agencies into disaster relief may seem logical and even desirable to ensure continuity between an emergency and what precedes or follows. There is an advantage to already being on the ground should a disaster strike because agencies have established long-term relationships. When Cyclone Nargis hit Burma, for example, the ICRC, MSF, and Oxfam were engaged in development activities and could quickly move into action. At the same time, this kind of presence clearly also exerts pressure to expand institutional resources. Even without being cynical, as Michael Maren tells us, "Few NGOs have ever seen a contract they didn't like, or a problem they didn't believe they could solve."[24]

The lack of regulation also means that "market failures" leave gaps in the provision of particular goods in a crisis or the wholesale neglect of an ongoing emergency. Donors, be they public (bilateral or multilateral) or private (foundations and individuals but also operational NGOs that are conduits for public funds), contribute resources when disaster strikes; but they are almost always earmarked for particular activities, a specific crisis, and a limited duration. Why focus on building latrines, for example, which might very well save more lives in crises, rather than advocacy or peacebuilding, which bring in more funding?

If a high-profile action is in the limelight, it gets resources, while they may be lacking for other nagging but invisible or less glamorous crises. Following the generous initial outpouring of record-breaking amounts of funds for the tsunami victims of December 2004, for instance, a chorus of familiar worries arose about sustained funding.[25] The likely results of waning public attention had a familiar ring for those seeking resources for war-torn societies. "Loud" emergencies, as long as they remain in the media spotlight, attract resources. But once they become "silent" and out of the headlines, resources evaporate or are in short supply. Even former "loud" crises such as Somalia do not endlessly echo and often further fundraising requires a new disaster like the famine of 2011–12 to once again shine the spotlight on the plight of those fleeing famine, pirates, or Al-Shabab.

Collective action dilemmas result because it is always possible to locate some NGOs that are willing to compete and deliver what a donor desires. To abstain from a particular area of operations or to avoid funds from a particular donor, for example, is a fairly hollow threat in a marketplace brimming with competitors – as possible funders or deliverers.

Humanitarian action reflects a value system, true, but it also is a product; and despite well-deserved accolades for their dedication and selflessness, aid agencies are also producers of services for hire. In the tussle for resources, not-for-profit aid agencies have felt the pressure to cater to donor interests in the pursuit of contracts that could be awarded to competitors or even to for-profit firms.[26] David Rieff denounces humanitarians for the willingness to permit donors to "hijack" the agenda, but individual organizations fret that too few resources make them ineffective and unable to take advantage of economies of scale.[27]

The internal debate is no longer, if it ever was, about whether to participate in the market but rather how and to what extent. "Dining with the devil" is an apt metaphor for it is only the duration and quality of such meals that varies agency by agency, and crisis by crisis. Few humanitarian organizations have consciously gone on a diet or fasted, although some religious pacifists (e.g., the Quakers, Mennonites, and Unitarians) have kept their distance from such repasts and the compromises required. As in the contemporary world more generally, however, we can find countervailing trends, and essays in an edited collection by Michael Barnett and Janice Stein call into question the distinction between "secular" and "sacred."[28] Meanwhile, Hugo Slim counsels the obvious need to compromise: "To get things done you will have to be tactical, make hard choices and form operational relationships that you would rather avoid."[29]

Cooley and Ron have argued persuasively that the contract culture of much of the humanitarian business is "deeply corrosive" of the humanitarian soul.[30] However, with hundreds of competitors, refusing to bid for a particular contract may have no impact other than the retention of a clear conscience – although maintaining "autonomy" by abstaining has become the justification for MSF's occasionally answering "no" to the question, "*Agir à tout prix?* (Acting at any price?)."[31]

Stories abound, for example, about those agencies assisting in the aftermath of the Rwandan genocide that sought to withdraw from a situation that seemed to be making matters worse. If a new contract or an extension of an old one is paramount, however, it becomes problematic to refuse to recognize or even accede to aberrant demands by warring parties and donors alike. If one agency refuses to respond to an unequivocal demand that violates all of its principles and also may make matters worse, just saying "no" may not actually be an option because there will be plenty of competitors willing to say "yes." Defection from an operation thus can seem and actually be pointless because another organization will rush in to carry out the role abandoned or not pursued.

Third, since donors' interests fluctuate with electoral results as well as with fads and publicity, aid agencies are obliged to dedicate institutional energies to currying favor with a wide array of funders. "Product differentiation" can be essential. Despite sharing many values, NGOs and UN agencies are often obliged to define themselves in contrast to what competing agencies offer. Having the image of being unusually capable in a sector constitutes a form of "branding." Resources being used for public relations and massaging donors, moreover, cannot be devoted to analyzing particular crises or designing better-adapted projects and programs.

While an earlier era may have made good use of well-intentioned volunteers and trained them on the spot, the top officials in major NGOs now have MBAs with a good understanding of business economics and are conversant with such topics as client relations, product positioning, human relations, accounting, and proposal writing. They have to be. Humanitarianism is a big business. Securing new and enlarged sources of support is an ever-expanding part of the central management function of aid agencies, leaving less time or energy to confront basic questions of ethics or efficiency.

Ensuring unity is problematic because humanitarian organizations often have mixed feelings for one another as well as genuine ideological differences over agendas, priorities, and the relevance of particular donor preferences. Again, decentralization and incentives to play along are not unique to today's wars, but their impact is dramatic because of the magnitude of funds available and the possibilities for manipulation and disruption. Humanitarians face pressure to act – from the collective conscience driven by the media as well as from funding sources that have their own targets to meet. Institutional rivalries raise the cost of doing business economically and politically. In the former we should include bidding wars for access, and in the latter undermining the effectiveness of operations and collective decision-making. Both erode respect for the humanitarian business and its employees.

Conclusion

The dynamics of particular humanitarian crises vary from one landscape to another, creating a range of demands. But many of the same suppliers come to the rescue depending on the incentives and disincentives operating in the humanitarian marketplace. Describing the current international humanitarian system as "unregulated" is an understatement.

None of the gamut of humanitarian actors can be satisfied with past performance, and many are in fact reviewing activities and rethinking shibboleths. Rather than the "me-first" approach inherent in the incentives and structure of the current system, the most obvious question that comes to mind is, "Would the international humanitarian system function better if organizations worked collectively instead of as competitors in such an unruly free market?"

The notion that somehow the dynamism and decentralization of the humanitarian family outweigh the disadvantages of centralization and integration has been a doubtful proposition for many years. In today's turbulence and in light of the size of the business, such atomization is unacceptable and unnecessary. While the successes of the enterprise in saving lives have been numerous and notable, so too have been the failures. In particular, competition for resources in an unregulated marketplace does not really make the survivors more efficient and effective in some modified Darwinian manner. It does, however, result in the increase in suppliers as well as in staff devoted to "selling" particular organizations. The dysfunctional humanitarian family has been struggling for some time, papering over differences and ignoring critical problems.

Notwithstanding a new sensitivity to the sector's short-comings and occasional efforts at reform, we have already encountered some additional distortions in the marketplace that skew humanitarian action. We now turn our attention to these acute problems.

CHAPTER FOUR

Market Distortions from Above and Below

This chapter confronts head-on several of the acute problems tormenting humanitarians as a result of manipulation by donors, belligerents, criminal elements, and merchants, as well as the unintended distortions of local economies generated by the very presence of aid agencies themselves. We have already encountered numerous contexts within which organizations find themselves wading in murky ethical waters. There are additional complications resulting from waste, inefficiency, and corruption. Other topics that enter an introductory economics course also come to the fore, namely what are often called "black" (or parallel) markets in which "taxation" and other dubious payments to belligerents often are viewed as the "normal" cost of doing business. The manipulation and diversion of aid is not a minor but rather a central problem for contemporary humanitarian action.

The Bilateralization of Aid

Accompanying the expansion in available resources elaborated in Chapter 2, donors have increasingly attached conditions to how those resources can be used. Multilateral aid (e.g., through the UN system) supposedly gives IGOs discretion over how the money is spent. However, it would be naïve to think that UN organizations could disregard the expressed preferences of major donor states or that ECHO would turn a deaf ear to its major contributing members. That is, instead of setting the agenda, aid agencies are often con-tractors for the national priorities of donors or recipients. But donor preferences are clearly articulated and affect the bottom line whereas those of recipients are tough to gauge and often are less consequential for the resource base.[1]

Particular donor countries can apply leverage and dictate to a multilateral organization either how money should be spent, or how it should be subcontracted to local or interna-tional NGOs. Earmarking is a practice by which the donor dictates where and how assistance may be used, frequently specifying priorities for regions, countries, operations, or even single projects; this approach is especially prominent if a government has geopolitical interests to protect or domes-tic constituencies to satisfy. Selling a Volvo to a recipient of Swedish aid is easier than selling a Toyota or Ford. In theory, such constraints apply less to IGOs than to bilateral aid agen-cies, but again only the naïve would ignore the interests of donors.

Over the last two or three decades, as states have pursued a neoliberal agenda, increasing contracts rather than expand-ing unrestricted programmatic commitments, there has been a dual shift that is unsettling to many humanitarians: away from multilateral toward bilateral aid as well as away from untied grants toward earmarking.[2] In 1988, states directed roughly 45 percent of humanitarian assistance through UN agencies. After 1994, however, the average dropped to 25 per-cent (and even lower in 1999 because of Kosovo).[3] A decade later, the trend continued downward, albeit more slowly, toward 11 percent, with only some $913 million of totally un-earmarked multilateral funds of the total of $8.7 billion in 2007's humanitarian expenditures.[4]

Whereas funding once allowed greater flexibility in the use of resources to accomplish an agency's own mission – including, on occasion, some risk-taking experiments – it is now increasingly earmarked for specific activities identified by a government funding source even when channeled through multilateral and nongovernmental organizations. The phenomenon is captured in the term "bilateralization." Among other implications of subcontracting their services, humanitarians are obliged to make even tougher decisions about establishing priorities for the increasingly small pool of unrestricted monies. Indeed, NGO decision-makers and managers have always placed a high priority on raising such funds because they are essential for discretionary spending: that is, decided upon by the agency and not the funding source. Although they may help to provide succor in an emergency, they also are useful for institutional growth: to pay for administrative costs that most public donors are loath to offset, to build up a donor base for future appeals, and to help leverage funds from other sources that require matching resources.

An intriguing question is the extent to which the lesser bilateralism and greater multilateralism of humanitarian aid reflected the fact that it suited governments, and especially Washington, to finance such assistance as a substitute for more robust political action. The growing "instrumentalization" (i.e., manipulation by donor governments as well as belligerents) may signal not the end of the putative golden age but rather the start of clarity about humanitarianism's purpose as viewed by states and political authorities, both donor and recipient. "With the end of the Cold War, with the increased involvement of Western troops in distant complex emergencies," Ian Smillie contends, "it could be argued that the reassertion of direct forms of political control over humanitarian action has become more evident, and perhaps more profound."[5]

Although these shifts may reflect the desire by member states to exert pressure and reduce perceived ineffectiveness by UN and other multilateral agencies, it is more plausible that donors wish to ensure more compatibility between donations and their own priorities. Accordingly, the needs of affected populations may take a back seat to donor-state interests in determining funding decisions. For instance, of the top 50 recipients of bilateral assistance between 1996 and 1999, the states of the former Yugoslavia, Israel/Palestine, and Iraq received 50 percent of the available resources.[6] By contrast, in 2000, the DRC ranked as the country with the lowest level of needs met – a mere 17.2 percent of its Consolidated Appeals Process (CAP); four years later it was Zimbabwe at 14.2 percent. The impact of 9/11 already was obvious in 2002 as nearly half of all funds given by donor governments to the UN's 25 appeals for assistance went to Afghanistan.[7] A decade later, the appeal for Afghanistan remained among the best-funded in proportion to requirements. Unsurprisingly, in the wake of the 2011 intervention to oust Gaddafi, Libya was also among the better funded CAPs. Sudan, Sri Lanka, and Haiti rounded out the top five, while the most underfunded included West Africa, Zimbabwe, and Djibouti.[8]

As could be expected, there is little difference between Western and non-OECD or non-traditional donors when it comes to the preference for bilateral over bilateralized multilateral channels. The geopolitical calculations of donors often trump basic humanitarian values.

Local War and Aid Economies

Textbooks about business economics make room for various types of distortions, including a frontier mentality and corruption. In war zones, however, the abnormal may often be normal, or certainly widespread, and the costs of doing humanitarian business may be so high as to call into question the entire undertaking. We encountered this reality as an element of so-called new wars in Chapter 2, but it is so important and so distorts the marketplace that it is discussed in greater depth here.

Nonstate actors come in various shapes, sizes, and sensibilities. Because many have economic interests that are served by continued violence, a host of distinctive dilemmas arise for aid agencies in war zones. While spoilers have been present in many previous armed conflicts, the current generation is more numerous and decentralized as well as better equipped to wreak havoc. The synergy of local and global economic conditions coupled with relatively inexpensive arms permits NSAs to assemble military capacity without much difficulty or investment; and groups and sub-groups can proliferate easily. Laurent Kabila reportedly said that to have an "army" in Central Africa, the price of entry into the market was cheap: $10,000 and a cell phone. Many NSAs are astute businesspeople who use economic means and have economic ends: that is, they exploit the production of violence and benefit from available resources. In the most perverse contexts, rebel groups and corrupt government officials, seemingly on opposing sides of a conflict, engage in "cooperative plunder," as the case of Angola illustrates.[9]

Two general types of economies influence war and humanitarian action. First are "war economies," or economic interests that directly profit from armed conflict, and second are the peculiarities of aid economies.

War Economies

In his farewell speech in 1961, US president Dwight D. Eisenhower warned about the "need to guard against the acquisition of unwarranted influence ... by the 'military-industrial complex.'"[10] Insurgents obviously do not operate with the sophistication in organization or technology of the US military-industrial complex, but a similarity is that both reward networks of economically calculating actors who profit from the production of violence.

Mark Duffield, in his study of "war economies," has termed the commercialization of political struggle "post-nation-state conflict." Globalization and liberalization, he argues, facilitate the procurement of arms and the establishment of parallel and trans-border economic linkages that are necessary for warring parties to sustain themselves. Market deregulation, structural adjustment, and the declining competence of the state "have not only allowed the politics of violence and profit to merge," he asserts, "but also underpin the regional trend toward protracted instability, schism, and political assertiveness in the [global] South."[11]

Conventional international relations theory tells us that the control of territory is essential to maintaining political authority, but the political economies in contemporary wars often impel actors to concentrate their energies on controlling commerce in a few resources, such as diamonds or tropical timber, rather than territory. Commercial activity in many of today's wars is premised on the continuation of violent conflict or is used to fuel it, or both. A form of criminal, distorting, and debilitating commerce is often the product of the exploitation of natural resources by private interests. Sometimes the formal economy of the state is manipulated for private gain – an "economy of plunder."[12] At other times, criminals, especially those operating as part of transnational networks, foster the erosion of state power to prevent traditional governmental regulation and taxation.[13] The opportunities for personal rewards and a means to finance war lead many NSAs to focus their efforts on securing access to natural resources, which frequently results in still more violence and heightened humanitarian crises. An analytical challenge arises in that it is extremely difficult to distinguish between those who use a political cause as a disguise to pursue criminal activities and those who pursue crime to raise money for a political cause; for our purposes, this is a distinction without a difference.

Despite the obvious economic advantages inherent in rich resource endowments, the armed conflicts that occur as a result of struggles over their control – what Michael Klare calls "resource wars"[14] – may be fundamentally disadvantageous. Indra de Soysa uses the expression "resource curse" to describe how abundant mineral wealth correlates with a greater frequency of economically based conflicts.[15] Examples of natural resources that fall into this schema and have financed the newest generation of wars include minerals (diamonds, cobalt, bauxite, gold, and oil) and agricultural commodities (tropical hardwoods and certain fruits and vegetables).[16] In an oft-cited World Bank study of conflicts from 1960 to 1995 that involved "natural resource predation," Paul Collier found that countries with such "lootable resources" were four times more likely to experience war than were those without them.[17]

Why is this important to humanitarians? Powerful external commercial interests that are vital to development – such as oil, mining, and timber companies – can sometimes constitute additional obstacles to relief efforts or even spark armed conflicts that trigger humanitarian crises. They contribute to the entrenchment of corruption and violence – either directly through illegal payments to bureaucrats that are often required for doing business, or passively by simply providing revenues that line the pockets of officials for whom "war is the end game." Foreign oil companies in Africa alone – whether operating in the "scorched earth" area of what is now South Sudan or in the charged ethnic environment of the river delta of Nigeria – demonstrate the significance of their impact on local economies and governance. Money paid by oil companies for signature bonuses to the Angolan government was even linked to weapons purchases, including landmines and cluster bombs.[18] Mining interests in the Congo, Sierra Leone, and Indonesia typify how large multinational corporations become powerbrokers in resource-rich countries. While oil represents the most substantial loot, other natural resources still account for non-trivial funds – illicit diamonds in Angola are believed to generate some $700 million per year and in Sierra Leone probably $350 million.[19]

Moreover, community grievances have been fueled in some instances by human rights abuses perpetrated by TNC-contracted security forces – whether a host country's armed forces or police (e.g., government forces purportedly acting to protect oil companies such as Shell in the Niger Delta), paramilitary groups, or private providers.[20] Security forces themselves have had an interest in sustaining conflict. In Sierra Leone, for example, mining companies (as well as the government) paid private military companies in return for mining rights. As Chantal de Jonge Oudraat asserts, "Of course, this makes these private military corporations more than simple hirelings; it makes them active actors in the conflicts in question. Ominously, they may actually profit from dragging out and escalating such conflicts."[21]

Humanitarians should understand that war directly benefits many persons – from NSAs to private security providers to even corrupt government officials – and that ending violence might very well destroy their base of power and source of wealth. This reality was partially obfuscated during the Cold War because local wars were overshadowed by larger strategic concerns pitting the two superpowers against each other and their allies.[22] Two researchers have summarized the analytical shift during the post-Cold War era from an initial focus on "economic deprivation or scarcity to an examination of the conflict-promoting aspects of resource abundance."[23] Although we learned earlier that many observers dispute that there is much new in the so-called new wars, there are certainly unfamiliar challenges within the humanitarian marketplace, where greed and grievance are commonplace,[24] and where the origins of exploitation may be very local.

Fledgling international responses to war economies follow two tracks: controlling means and controlling ends. The former approach seeks to prevent or limit economically based actors from developing the means to wage war through such international efforts as restricting the spread of small arms and banning mercenaries. Several studies have spotlighted the former, and humanitarians have worked to limit the production and distribution of these weapons by targeting arms sales.[25]

The second track seeks to regulate the resources over which warring parties struggle. The UN has attempted to control the role of the plunder of natural resources, with particular emphasis on Africa.[26] A variety of lootable resources play an enormous role in sustaining wars, and codes of conduct are becoming increasingly important in the diamond industry. The Kimberley process began in May 2000 with a meeting in South Africa after NGOs such as Global Witness pressured the diamond industry to accept regulation and clamp down on an illicit trade responsible for fueling wars.[27] The Kimberley Certification Scheme came into effect on January 1, 2003 to control trade in over 40 countries. However, many diamond operations were not covered by this agreement and thus it was supplemented in August 2005 by the Diamond Development Initiative, within which NGOs, multinational diamond companies, and governments work together to expand the scope of the program. This, though, has had limited results and many leakages, such as in Zimbabwe, which in December 2011 led Global Witness to pull out of the scheme that it helped pioneer.[28]

Aid Economies

The second general type of economic exploitation is more peculiar but also more pertinent for our assessment of today's war zones, namely local "aid economies," the local economic interests that exploit the provision of external resources designed to help the helpless. The focus is not so much on benefiting from violence but rather on taking advantage of efforts to relieve the suffering caused by violence. More violence means more suffering and more succor with more opportunities to profit.

Aid agencies have long sought to find ways to avoid the manipulation of markets that benefits profiteers and fosters dependency. Providing aid can facilitate exploitation by creating greedy intermediaries, speculation, and hoarding as well as generate conditions conducive to breeding future resentments and exacerbating local tensions. Furthermore, outside aid can also be an unfortunate disincentive to the creation and development of sustainable indigenous institutions.

Humanitarians are often thrust into uncertain political territory populated by a wide array of actors. They focus on populations at risk, but other actors are just as important. Efforts to recognize this reality tend to paint all participants with too broad brush-strokes that often disguise the essence of the problem – rarely are the binary distinctions as clear-cut as "good guys" vs. "bad guys."

Unpacking the politics of war-torn societies reveals a three-fold problem for those outside aid workers within the marketplace. The first is identifying, engaging, and promoting those actors that facilitate humanitarian operations, contribute to reconstruction efforts, and support peacebuilding – in short, nurturing civil society and peace-oriented actors. The second is limiting relations with and curtailing the influence of rogues who profit politically or economically from war – marginalizing and navigating "uncivil" society or such spoilers as warlords and mafiosi. The third is distinguishing those who have the potential to contribute to humanitarian action but may not readily do so, and finding strategies and tactics with appropriate incentives for transforming their interest structures toward fostering peace or at least not continuing to wreak havoc in order to secure an income.

It is virtually impossible not to work with "spoilers,"[29] but humanitarians have to pay particular attention to minimize the chances that they may inadvertently enhance the legitimacy of illegitimate actors. Formal relations with spoilers implicitly acknowledge their authority; and a relief role can bolster claims to legitimacy.[30] This problem was less acute, or perhaps more awkward and less frequent, for UN organizations before civil wars and NSAs became so widespread. For instance, in the 1980s, UNICEF was chosen to lead Operation Lifeline Sudan because women and children, the focus of that organization, were deemed exceptional, and so its dealing with the Sudanese Liberation Army did not necessarily imply international recognition, which would have been the case for involvement by other international organizations.[31] At present, few barriers to entry exist to prevent humanitarians from entering the marketplace in war zones, and virtually all UN organizations and a gaggle of NGOs vie for a fair share of that market. Helping affected populations immediately usually takes precedence over possible downstream problems of unpalatable partners, and this dynamic complicates calculating the true costs and benefits.

There are numerous illustrations of direct and indirect attempts to thwart the efforts of humanitarian workers in aid economies from conflict zones around the world. During the Second Liberian Civil War (1999–2003), for instance, warlord Charles Taylor – subsequently sentenced in The Hague for war crimes – demanded 15 percent of aid entering territory that he controlled. Estimates of the proportion of aid looted, diverted, and extorted in Somalia in the 1990s reached as high as 80 percent on the territory of certain warlords, while at least 50 percent of all food aid in Bosnia was used to feed and supply combatants.[32] Aid diversion empowers those responsible for the bloodshed; and feeding killers in militarized camps threatens civilian refugees and IDPs in addition to further enabling violence. Paying a "tax" to those who control access allows humanitarians to assist victims, but simultaneously such a practice fosters continued violence by belligerents.

What exactly is the root of the problem? Humanitarian aid can relieve belligerents of some of the administrative and financial burdens of waging war, effectively increasing their capacity to continue fighting by diminishing the demands of governing and cutting the costs of sustaining casualties. The list of examples is depressingly long. For instance, in the Horn of Africa in the 1980s and 1990s, famines attracted outside food aid that allowed governments and insurgents to feed fighters who continued to slaughter targeted groups. Taking care of refugees whose population included killers in the 1980s in Cambodia and in the 1990s and 2000s in the DRC had an unexpected result: the insurgents were able to regroup and pursue their policies of extermination and rape – and in the DRC, that reality still continues.

Perhaps the most significant manifestation of what would usually be called corruption but is now a cost of business in war zones consists of purchasing access through payments to those who control territory. Central government authorities and warlords both try to siphon off as large a portion of the value of aid supplies as they can. Earlier we mentioned estimates ranging from 15 to 80 percent; a "tax" of 25–30 percent seems to be a working average, this being the share both that Indonesian soldiers claimed from the 2004 tsunami relief in Aceh, where a guerrilla group had been operating and where humanitarians were keen to have access after years of isolation, and that Serbian soldiers claimed from the UNHCR throughout the former Yugoslavia in the 1990s.[33]

The names given to such payments can vary, restricted only by the creativity of the wordsmiths demanding payments from aid workers. They include fees for visas, passes, and work permits; import duties on aid supplies; fees for airports, harbors, and border crossings; registration fees for cars and trucks along with tolls for road usage; and sales and income taxes. Such mild forms of extortion, or even more blatant ones for "protection insurance," improve access to vulnerable populations, to be sure, but they also go straight into the war chests or pockets of belligerents.

Another reality within the marketplace results because UN organizations and international NGOs are practically the only source of employment. When unemployment is universal and people are desperate for work to feed their families, external aid agencies may constitute virtually the entire formal monetized sector. International salaries paid regularly and in foreign exchange are attractive not only to professionals, technicians, and those with language skills to communicate with locals but also to drivers, guards, gardeners, and maids. Stories of manual laborers working for external agencies who earn 10 times the salary of senior government officials highlight the problems of skewed incentives in aid economies. With remuneration that is 10 to 30 times as high as the equivalent position in the local economy, it is hardly surprising that hundreds of applicants may appear for any vacancy posted by aid agencies.

While this may not seem startling to the reader who is accustomed to fluid labor markets, it can sometimes have disastrous consequences for the longer-run health of war-torn societies. The shift of skilled personnel away from the productive sector or from the government to the humanitarian marketplace means a loss for the local economy that often is permanent as employees may well wish to continue working inside aid agencies or to emigrate. Moreover, if hiring procedures are perceived to have been unfair, aid agencies can be confronted with spurned applicants and their family members. In other cases, local staff who are fired or whose contracts are not renewed also can become security problems as they seek to bite or retaliate against the hand that once fed them.

One relatively recent phenomenon revolves around setting up bogus local nonprofit counterparts, which can be little more than institutional fronts for rogues. They are often created to satisfy the demand for "local control" emanating from outside donors who wish to be politically correct. Yet what has been cynically dubbed a "Doxfam" (donor-created Oxfam) or an "UNONGO" (UN-organized NGO), for instance, is not a genuine local product but rather an attempt to "capture" agencies, monopolize jobs and resources, and prevent assistance from being distributed to adversaries. In the worst cases, external agencies inadvertently become a virtual logistical support unit for militias.

Local administrators or armed belligerents also profit in such distorted economies by manipulating exchange rates: for instance, insisting upon payments in typically highly inflated "official" exchange rates, which provide for a huge profit margin when actually exchanging currency on the parallel market. Other forms of remuneration that count as distortions include providing access to local contacts for important construction and other supplies, travel abroad, per diem payments, and favorable sales of rented property and vehicles. The benefits thus do not go to viable businesses but to cronies. Armed belligerents, including child soldiers, moreover, are essentially "employed";[34] without education or viable job opportunities, war makes sense to them as individual wage-earners and perhaps to their families, who benefit.

Reliable figures are extremely difficult to compile for these types of distortions, although virtually every aid worker could provide a litany of anecdotes. Empirical evidence would provide ammunition to those in Western parliaments keen to cut overseas aid, and so little effort is made to document abuses. Nevertheless, humanitarian organizations find themselves unusually vulnerable to such exploitation. In comparison with earlier periods in humanitarian history, and to reiterate a theme from the previous chapter, the proliferation of agencies in the post-Cold War era makes it easier for belligerents to exploit rivalries and harder for aid organizations to mount a united front or to withdraw.

Local commercial interests constitute a blend of promise and pitfall that is pivotal in shaping the operating environment for humanitarians. Profiteers manipulate markets to benefit from the high prices common in aid economies.[35] Necessities such as grain and gasoline are "priced" to account for the expense of production and distribution but have also been inflated to enrich speculators and intermediaries ("middlemen"). Merchants and traders are stakeholders in the price of basic commodities, which can be undermined by the availability of relief goods in local markets. Private sector providers of key services in veterinary medicine, vaccinations and health care, agricultural supplies, and even potable water see profits dwindle when aid agencies provide goods for free. Well-intentioned relief can make enemies of legitimate local businesspeople, prompting them to sabotage wells, drive food convoys away, or even incite violence against aid agencies. To counteract this, one of the more astute measures used in Somalia in 1993, for example, was to make foodstuffs commercially available, rather than free, which forced hoarders to dump their commodities and which enticed legitimate traders back into business.[36] Similarly, the ICRC cooked rice supplies to decrease their economic value and inhibit predatory economic behavior such as reselling foodstuffs.

To add to the list of possible woes, humanitarian organizations have also been taken to task as the primary beneficiaries of aid economies, helping to perpetuate the kind of misery that they are supposed to redress. When operating expenses – including such big-ticket items as salaries, transportation, equipment, housing, insurance, and security – rival the aid delivered or when international aid workers live lives of luxury next door to feeble shanties and squalid refugee camps, the humanitarian enterprise not only appears to waste scarce resources but also tarnishes its reputation. Alex de Waal, William Shawcross, and Michael Maren are among those who stridently criticize outside humanitarian agencies as enriching themselves from the needs of local populations on the dole.[37] Their criticisms revolve around many of the factors indicated above that upend local markets, fortify war-makers, and create yet new crises for victims. If chaos continues long enough, relief aid weakens local capacities and undermines authority structures. In fact, to put their critique starkly, humanitarianism can be as damaging as colonialism.

There is the possibility that states and deeper structural imperatives made humanitarians enlarge the scope of their activities beyond the provision of immediate assistance to victims of war and of natural disasters. Aid worker-turned-academic Mark Duffield argues that broader discourses of security, liberalism, and development have shaped what humanitarianism is and what it does. In other words, it is implicated in a broader set of global discourses. He actually goes a step further and lambasts Western aid agencies because they require wars as part of a new international political economy; armed conflicts give humanitarians a *raison d'être* and produce additional funding.[38] Such thoughts do not have to lead to the sort of conspiracy-theory arguments best associated with Noam Chomsky – in which humanitarianism is nothing more than an instrument of imperial design – though they often do. Cynics and even reformed aid workers like Tony Vaux argue that the dominant focus of humanitarianism is not on those who receive aid but on the virtue of those who give it.[39] A more reasonable view is that we can appreciate the global forces that are shaping humanitarianism's character without succumbing to an overly simplistic and reductionist view that humanitarianism is nothing more than the fumes of power.

Among humanitarians the response to the above litany of distortions has not quite been to throw up collective arms in despair but rather to pursue a modified Hippocratic oath. The consequences of ignoring or eroding local capacities has long been a theme in Mary Anderson's work,[40] which has led to the adoption of "do-no-harm" criteria in aid manuals and operations. The idea behind such efforts is to design emergency efforts in a fashion that minimizes their negative consequences and aims to improve the ability of communities and public authorities to take control of their own destinies, begin development, and be in a position to react better to future disasters. In the do-no-harm approach, preserving or facilitating local capacity development helps determine how humanitarian relief resources are allocated. Applying such an approach requires a detailed knowledge of local culture and economics as well as a discipline that is hard to come by in the rough-and-tumble circumstances of contemporary humanitarian calamities.

This discussion of local war and aid economies suggests the uncertain and shaky terrain on which aid agencies walk while trying to help. The changes in war and politics and humanitarian practice mean that the position of humanitarians is not safely insulated as it once was. "Humanitarian action is under attack, but neither governments, parties to armed conflicts, nor other influential actors are doing enough to come to its relief," a 2011 OCHA report argues.[41]

Again, while many elements were present in the armed conflicts of earlier historical periods, the magnitude of outside
aid and the existence of a globalizing world economy create
an unusual witches' brew of challenges for humanitarians in
today's marketplace.

Conclusion

What is the cumulative impact of these market distortions?
Skewed resource allocation aligned with the interests of
donors and sometimes belligerents and criminal groups. The
power of resources is such that few agencies can be cavalier
and ignore donor dictates, while belligerent control of access
means that agencies often have to bargain with unsavory local
actors.

Arguably the most important control mechanism from
donors comes from the power of the purse, and state interests affect the pattern of giving – or, rather, determine whose
suffering matters. Most humanitarian organizations are
highly dependent on government funding, and states can
use this dependency to their advantage. Donors can make
threats to influence how agencies behave. In 2003, USAID
administrator Andrew Natsios was rumored to have told
humanitarian organizations operating in Iraq that they were
obligated to show the American flag if they were recipients of
US funding. If they refused to do so, he supposedly warned
them, they could be replaced.[42] One NGO official captured
Washington's message: "[P]lay the tune or 'they'll take you out
of the band.'"[43] It turns out that the Natsios story was apocry-
phal, and his statement never occurred. However, that it was
believed and believable says something about the climate of
the times and the collective state of mind in agencies operating in the humanitarian marketplace. As the president of
the French section of MSF straightforwardly comments,

"[T]he political exploitation of aid is not a misuse of its vocation, but its principal condition of existence."[44]

The bilateralization of aid and earmarking of funds not only have channeled efforts by individual agencies but also have led to new trends in overall allocations. Again, we should recall that multilateral aid is often considered superior because technically it is defined as aid handed over to IGOs so that these organizations determine how the money is spent. In contrast to multilateral aid, bilateral aid is earmarked, which means that the donor state dictates to funding recipients how the money is to be spent, including specifying a particular geographic region or even pet projects to benefit constituents back home. State interests, rather than the principle of relief based on an objective assessment of need, increasingly drive all funding decisions. In general, while there are more humanitarian dollars and euros than ever before, they are controlled by fewer donors that are more inclined to impose conditions and direct aid toward their own priorities. A several-tiered system means that the least fortunate often get the least attention. In response to the politicization of priorities, humanitarian organizations entered into a dialogue with the principal donors to try to establish more impartial standards, resulting in was called the Good Donorship Initiative; this, however, has yet to move beyond the rhetoric of less donor and more humanitarian priorities.[45]

The marketplace responds to burgeoning vulnerable populations on the shifting political and institutional sands of collapsing states that are unable to provide food, shelter, sanitation, health care, and physical protection. Humanitarians encounter not only the traditional challenges of emergency relief (mustering political will and resources to respond, and complementing other recovery efforts beyond the emergency stage), but also extra hazards inherent in "stateless" complex emergencies: violence and the extreme politicization of aid.

The modern international humanitarian system, inadequately funded and originally designed to address natural disasters and interstate conflicts, is now plagued by additional complications associated with the specific horrors of state failure and grisly civil wars, including armed actors who do not respect the laws of war and may actually profit from its perpetuation.

CHAPTER FIVE

The Push and Pull of Coming to the Rescue

This chapter returns to two topics that have made brief appearances but merit fuller treatment because of their impact on the character of the contemporary marketplace. The first concerns the impact of the terrorist attacks of September 11, 2001, and the ensuing war on terror on the nature of humanitarian action. This exogenous shock contrasts with the second, an endogenous event within international society: the responsibility to protect (R2P), which many observers – friends and foes alike – consider the fastest moving. Both will help to shed light on the unevenness in world responses to crises, by governments and humanitarians, and on the choice of high-profile emergencies over less publicized and less popular ones. This chapter makes apparent that although market forces are not drivers of military intervention in the same way that they influence humanitarian action, military intervention creates new markets for the humanitarian business and its shareholders.

Post-9/11 Politics

The main driving force for development and humanitarian aid during the Cold War was geopolitical. Financing helped European countries retain a say in their former colonies, and Moscow and Washington engaged in a competition for influence. With the fall of the Berlin Wall, the ideological struggle ended, and much of the justification for assistance evaporated: for example, flows from the United States, France, and the United Kingdom fell by half in the first part of the 1990s. The onslaught of civil wars in the same period changed the justification for official aid toward a more people-centered solidarity. While it is an exaggeration to state that 9/11 changed everything, the fateful attacks certainly suggested the intimate security link between developed countries and weak states; and so additional resources were poured into the Afghanistans, Yemens, and Iraqs of this world. And the beneficiaries of these resources included aid agencies and PMSCs.

Complex humanitarian emergencies have regional and sometimes global consequences, which reinforces the close relationship between domestic and international order, between the push and pull of the competing priorities, between national security and traditional humanitarian values. Michael Ignatieff, for one, pointed to "bad neighborhoods" such as Afghanistan and Sudan, which offered fertile soil for international terrorists. They served as breeding grounds for the perpetrators of the attacks on US embassies in East Africa in 1998, the USS *Cole* in Yemen in 2000, and US soil in September 2001.[1] Failed states seemed a threat not only to themselves but also to others. Hence, states and other international actors could not ignore them and, indeed, had a vested interest in "saving" them.[2]

In general, the more that states were willing to use funding to further their political interests, the more that aid agencies were willing to do what it took to keep on the good side of those with the money. States also began discovering ways that their security interests intersected with humanitarian action. In the post-9/11 global war on terror – in March 2009 conveniently relabeled the "overseas contingency operation" by the US Department of Defense – counterterrorism and humanitarianism, at least according to the United States and other major Western powers, have become partners.

Media-influenced perceptions can influence state military capacity by priming the pump for civilian participation. President Lyndon B. Johnson referred to the media campaign to foster US support for its South Vietnamese allies as a battle for "hearts and minds." Wars that are seen as being illegitimate or too costly can lessen popular support and weaken militaries from within, which is how the Vietnam War subsequently was at least partially "lost."

With failed states as sanctuaries and staging platforms for terrorists, humanitarian organizations can become part of wider hearts-and-minds campaigns, attempting to convince local populations of the goodness of armies invading in the name of stability and freedom. In his now famous or infamous words, US secretary of state Colin Powell told a gathering of private aid agencies that "just as surely as our diplomats and military, American NGOs are out there [in Afghanistan] serving and sacrificing on the frontlines of freedom. NGOs are such a force multiplier for us, such an important part of our combat team."[3]

Such logic was hardly unusual, but Powell's straightforward billing was far clearer than the packaging used by some of his predecessors. Humanitarians were force multipliers after World War II as well as in Korea, Vietnam (and elsewhere in Southeast Asia), Afghanistan, and Central America. However, no prior secretary of state thought that NGOs were important enough to address at a special gathering and enunciate clearly and without apology what everyone already knew, namely that humanitarians, in Antonio Donini's apt image, play second fiddle[4] and serve the interests of those who pay the bills.[5]

On the ground in Afghanistan and Iraq, the overwhelmingly top-down direction of operations and overly intimate relationship between humanitarian work and military and political operations was manifest in provincial reconstruction teams (PRTs). The blurred distinction between military and humanitarian actors raised concerns among agencies about their perceived lack of independence from the "occupiers" and hence their increased insecurity in these war-torn societies, a topic addressed extensively in Chapter 2. Save the Children, in an extensive report on humanitarian relief in Afghanistan, noted the dual problem with PRTs: the risk of aid agencies "being perceived as working directly with, or for, the military, and therefore being seen as legitimate targets in the ongoing conflict;" and their use as a substitute for enhancing security throughout the country.[6]

The extreme difficulty, if not to say impossibility, of isolating the political from the humanitarian in the UN's "integrated missions" was a major preoccupation in *The State of the World's Refugees 2012*: "Notwithstanding the efforts of UNHCR to be strictly apolitical, aid itself can be highly political."[7] Since the directions given in 2006 by UN secretary-general Kofi Annan,[8] the efforts of all UN organizations within a country are to be channeled in the same direction, namely to resolve the armed conflict and begin the process of peacebuilding. Clearly there is a tension between the humanitarian and the political, and it is the latter that predominates in such situations. How can one square the circle, or, in the UNHCR's view, attempt "not be perceived as aligned with political or security agendas"?[9]

States also bolstered humanitarian action in order to avoid or postpone more costly political decisions and actions. This policy approach is not new. Former US president Theodore Roosevelt responded to the decision by one of his successors, Woodrow Wilson, to steer clear of the 1915 Armenian genocide. "To allow the Turks to massacre the Armenians," he said, "and then solicit permission to help the survivors and then to allege the fact that we are helping the survivors as a reason why we should not follow the only policy that will permanently put a stop to such massacres is both foolish and odious."[10]

The fig leaves of the 1990s were labeled a "humanitarian alibi" by frustrated aid workers who felt that they were being manipulated by states. The former UN high commissioner for refugees, Sadako Ogata, for one, became an outspoken opponent of such contrivances by continually repeating: "There are no humanitarian solutions to humanitarian problems."[11] Mark Duffield has pointed out that viewing armed conflicts as having local causes – ethnicity, tribalism, and religion – serves a political purpose of legitimating a purely humanitarian response; it is thus easier to underplay the role of such exogenous forces as trade, colonialism, and inequality.[12] One need not agree with Duffield, who views humanitarian action as a means to maintain Western hegemony, in order to appreciate that it is easier to respond with humanitarian band-aids rather than intervene militarily or economically to address the root local or international causes of war, violence, exploitation, poverty, and terrorism.

Ogata once described herself as "the desk officer for the former Yugoslavia" because the major powers had authorized the UNHCR to deliver vast amounts of humanitarian relief in Bosnia, in part to relieve the growing pressure for a military intervention and a political commitment to finding a solution. Regardless of whether or not states possessed the right motives, they afforded new opportunities for relief and protection in areas that formerly had been largely off-limits for civilian humanitarians. Yet to the extent that it became a substitute for politics and a sop to hopeful publics, aid could, according to Alex de Waal, lead "Western governments and donating publics to be deluded into believing the fairy tale that their aid can solve profound political problems, when it cannot."[13] The war on terror since 9/11 has only made these realities starker.

Based on OECD/DAC and OCHA FTS data, the top recipients of aid between 2000 and 2009 suggest that money flows toward the favored geopolitical territories. Among the top five allocations by country were: Sudan ($8.9 billion); Palestine/ Occupied Palestinian Territories (OPT) ($7.2 billion); Iraq ($5.1 billion); Afghanistan ($5.1 billion); and Ethiopia ($4.8 billion). These top five recipients have been ranked among the top 10 for the past decade, alongside the DRC, Somalia, Pakistan, Indonesia, and Lebanon. It is notable that the DRC ranks sixth, given that it was considered the world's "forgotten emergency." However, the *GHA Report 2011* explains that the upswing is a result of a concerted NGO advocacy campaign along with changes in the UN's appeal process and funding architecture. Aid has in fact been increasingly concentrated in a smaller number of recipient countries over the past decade.

The United States is by far the largest provider of military humanitarian assistance; most of what is actually reported to OECD/DAC as ODA unsurprisingly has been channeled to Afghanistan and Iraq. This contains not only aid directly implemented by the US military but also its subcontracting to partners. As the *GHA Report 2011* asserts, "The humanitarian aid delivered by military actors that is reported as ODA corresponds closely with security crises where major donors have military personnel deployed."[14]

Responsibility to Protect

At numerous junctures in this volume we have encountered the "responsibility to protect." The task here is to understand better how it affects the push and pull between acting or standing on the sidelines by reframing the contested and counterproductive label of "humanitarian intervention."

Beginning with the international response in northern Iraq in 1991, this moniker had led to largely circular and futile tirades about the agency, timing, legitimacy, means, circumstances, and advisability of using military force to protect human beings. The politics of an agreement on this norm suggest the importance of humanitarians' not pretending to be above or beyond politics but rather being actively engaged in them.

With the exception of the efforts of Raphael Lemkin, lawyer and refugee from war-torn Poland, to advance the term "genocide" and an international legal ban against its practice – which came to fruition with the adoption of the 1948 Convention on the Prevention and Punishment of the Crime of Genocide – no idea has moved faster in the international normative arena than "the responsibility to protect" (R2P, or the uglier RtoP in current UN parlance), the title of the 2001 report from the International Commission on Intervention and State Sovereignty.[15] Proponents and critics have agreed that the commission's contribution to forestalling and stopping mass atrocities was its specific framework with a three-pronged responsibility: to prevent, react, and rebuild.

R2P's central normative tenet is that state sovereignty is contingent and not absolute; it thus entails duties not simply rights. After centuries of largely looking the other way, sovereignty no longer provides a license for mass murder in the eyes of legitimate members of the international community of states. Every state has a responsibility to protect its own citizens from mass killings and other gross violations of their rights. If any state, however, is manifestly unable or unwilling to exercise that responsibility, or actually is the perpetrator of mass atrocities, its sovereignty is abrogated. Meanwhile the responsibility to protect devolves to the international community of states, ideally acting through the UN Security Council.

This framework's dual responsibility – internal and external – draws upon work by Francis Deng and Roberta Cohen about "sovereignty as responsibility." The ICISS commissioners' report was poorly timed: although finalized in August 2011, it was not actually published until December, by which time, of course, 9/11 had occurred and so progress was temporarily sidetracked. However, the ideas in the report were revived and embraced later by over 150 heads of state and government at the UN's 2005 World Summit;[16] and the reframing moved away from humanitarian intervention as a "right." Deng, Cohen, ICISS, and the World Summit emphasized the need – indeed, the responsibility – for the international community of states, embodied by the United Nations and mandated since its creation to deliver FDR's "freedom from fear," to do everything possible to prevent mass atrocities. Deploying military force is an option after alternatives have been considered and failed. Military intervention to protect the vulnerable is restricted, in the summit's language, to cases of "genocide, war crimes, ethnic cleansing and crimes against humanity" – or the shorthand of "mass atrocity crimes."

Using military force *in extremis* with a view toward "saving strangers"[17] was the lynch-pin for the debate resulting from international inaction in 1994 in Rwanda (doing too little too late) and action in 1999 in Kosovo (according to some, doing too much too soon). The R2P agenda encompasses a host of responses to mass atrocities, ranging from prevention to post-conflict rebuilding, and not merely the use of overwhelming military force to stop them after they begin. The World Summit set aside peacebuilding (or included it as part of prevention, thereby downgrading it). But the full and distinct spectrum of prevention, reaction, and rebuilding remains a preferable conceptual framework. The integrity of the original ICISS conceptualization suffers when diluted or conflated so that prevention becomes an all-encompassing category without a meaningful policy edge.

Whether using the original ICISS conception or the 2005

World Summit version, two specific challenges remain. First, R2P should not become synonymous with everything that the United Nations does. In addition to reacting and protecting civilians at risk, the value added of R2P consists of proximate prevention and proximate peacebuilding: that is, efforts to move back from the brink of mass atrocities that have yet to become widespread or efforts after such crimes to ensure that they do not recur. International action is required before the only option is the US Army's 82nd Airborne Division; and additional commitments to help mend societies are also essential in order to avoid beginning anew a cycle of settling accounts and crimes.

However, the responsibility to protect is not about the protection of everyone from everything. Broadening perspectives has opened the floodgates to an overflow of appeals to address too many problems. For example, part of the political support at the World Summit reflected an understandable but erroneous desire to mobilize support for development to overcome root causes of conflict. As bureaucrats invariably seek justifications for pet projects, we run the risk that everything may figure on the R2P agenda. It is emotionally tempting to argue that we have a responsibility to protect people from HIV/AIDS, small arms, and global warming. However, if R2P means everything, it means nothing.

Conversely, the responsibility to protect also should not be viewed too narrowly. It is not *only* about the use of military force. The broad emphasis especially pertinent after Washington's and London's 2003 rhetoric disingenuously morphed into a vague "humanitarian" justification for the war in Iraq when weapons of mass destruction and links to Al-Qaeda proved non-existent. The Iraq war temporarily was a conversation stopper for R2P as critics looked askance upon the consideration of any humanitarian justification for military force. Contemporary foreign adventurism and imperial meddling in humanitarian guise are not more acceptable than earlier incarnations.

Yet R2P breaks new ground in coming to the rescue. In addition to the usual attributes of a sovereign state that students encounter in international relations and law courses and in the 1934 Montevideo Convention – people, authority, territory, and independence – there is another: a modicum of respect for basic human rights. The interpretation of privileges for sovereigns has made room for modest responsibilities as well. When a state is unable or manifestly unwilling to protect the rights of its population – and especially when it perpetuates abuse – that state loses its sovereignty along with the accompanying right of nonintervention. The traditional rule of noninterference in the internal affairs of other countries does not apply in the face of mass atrocities.

Moreover, the outdated discourse of humanitarian intervention is turned on its head and transformed from that properly detested in the global South. The merits of particular situations should be evaluated rather than blindly given an imprimatur as "humanitarian." For anyone familiar with the number of sins justified by that adjective during the heyday of colonialism, this change marks a profound shift away from the rights of outsiders to intervene toward the rights of populations at risk to assistance and protection and the responsibility of outsiders to help.

In what Gareth Evans calculates to be "a blink of the eye in the history of ideas,"[18] developments since the release of the ICISS report in December 2001 show that R2P has moved from the passionate prose of an international commission's report toward being a mainstay of international public policy debate. Edward Luck aptly reminds us that the lifespan of successful norms is "measured in centuries, not decades,"[19] but R2P seems firmly embedded in the values of international society and occasionally in policies and tactics for a particular crisis. And it certainly has the potential to evolve further in customary international law and to contribute to ongoing conversations about the qualifications of states as legitimate, rather than rogue, sovereigns.

Merely listing contemporary headlines is impressive. Prior to the World Summit's endorsement of R2P, in 2004 the UN's High-level Panel on Threats, Challenges and Change issued *A More Secure World: Our Shared Responsibility*, which supported "the emerging norm that there is a collective international responsibility to protect."[20] Kofi Annan endorsed it in his 2005 report, *In Larger Freedom*.[21] In addition to the official blessing by the UN General Assembly in October 2005, the Security Council had made references to R2P on several occasions: the April 2006 resolution 1674 on the protection of civilians in armed conflict expressly "reaffirms the provisions of paragraphs 138 and 139" and the August 2006 resolution 1706 on Darfur repeats the same language with specific reference to that conflict. The first meaningful operational references to the "responsibility to protect" came against Libya in 2011: resolution 1970 had unanimous support for a substantial package of Chapter VII efforts (arms embargo, asset freeze, travel bans, and reference of the situation to the International Criminal Court); and no state voted against resolution 1973, which authorized "all necessary measures" to enforce a no-fly zone and protect civilians. Subsequently in July 2011, in approving a peacekeeping mission in South Sudan, R2P once again figured in resolution 1996. In addition, the Human Rights Council referred to R2P for the first time in resolution S-15/1, which led to the General Assembly's resolution 65/60, which suspended Libyan membership in the council. In fact, 11 Security Council decisions have involved the R2P norm, with 6 of these taking place in 2011 alone – for South Sudan, Yemen, and Syria after Libya – and 1 in 2012.

UN administrative strengthening began in 2007 when UN secretary-general Ban Ki-moon appointed a special adviser for the prevention of genocide (Francis M. Deng and subsequently Adama Dieng in 2012) and another for promoting R2P (Edward C. Luck); and the General Assembly approved additional resources in 2010 for their joint office. Ban has referred to the implementation of R2P as one of his priorities, although tentativeness has characterized most of the UN's efforts under his tenure, by which he hopes to finesse controversy among reluctant Third World countries about what had launched the debate in the first place: the use of military force for human protection purposes.

The R2P norm has moved quickly, it is true, but the concept is still young, as Luck notes: "[L]ike most infants, R2P will need to walk before it can run."[22] The process begun by ICISS continues to be a cause for civil society, UN officials, and supportive governments that push skeptical countries and the UN bureaucracy to take seriously Ban's earlier rhetorical call to translate "words to deeds."[23]

The R2P norm has a clear potential pay-off for the humanitarian business. Military protection in contexts of mass atrocities will not only facilitate the work of humanitarians on the ground, but in some cases assistance – both logistical and security – from outside military forces will be the only way that humanitarians can reach suffering populations. In Darfur, for example, Khartoum restricted access to those in need. Similarly, in war-torn Somalia, Islamist insurgents, pirates, and thugs posed grave difficulties for those trying to reach famine victims; Al-Shabab, now publicly under the Al-Qaeda umbrella, even expelled 16 aid agencies, including UNICEF, from the large swaths of territory under its control in November 2011 when a quarter of a million Somalis remained at risk of starvation and another 1.4 million were displaced.

Conclusion: The Unevenness of Global Responses

The pushes and pulls highlighted by examining the impact of 9/11 help to shed light on the new rationales behind the unevenness in the world's responses to crises, by governments and humanitarians. There have always been discrepancies; aid flows to some countries dwarf those to others. But 9/11 demonstrates new reasons why states and humanitarians opt for high-profile emergencies over less publicized ones.

If funding decisions were based solely on need, then places such as the DRC, northern Uganda, and Angola would leapfrog to the top of the list. Evidence suggests, however, that in the 1990s such countries were neglected while the bulk of the resources went to the Balkans. This reality prompted then UN secretary-general Boutros Boutros-Ghali to call Bosnia "a white man's war," referring among other things to the fact that in per capita terms it was much more attractive to be a war victim resident in Europe than in Africa. Similarly, during the crisis in Kosovo in 1999, aid abundantly poured into this European region, with a "donor response [to the UN's CAP] for the former Yugoslavia [amounting to] $207 per person," while "for Sierra Leone, it was $16, and $8 for the Democratic Republic of the Congo."[24] In comparison, consolidated appeals for that year generated about $10 per capita for North Korea or Uganda but $185 for southeastern Europe.[25] Indeed, from 1993 to 2000 almost half of the funds from ECHO were disbursed in Europe. In another telling comparison, one analyst noted that "the money spent by the US Army/OFDA [Office of Foreign Disaster Assistance] on Camp Hope in Albania, which housed just over 3,000 people for two months, was roughly the same amount as the UN's entire annual appeal for Angola."[26]

Unsurprisingly, the top five underfunded appeals in early

2012 were for Liberia, Côte d'Ivoire, Haiti, the Central African Republic, and the Democratic Republic of the Congo.[27] The DRC – the world's most "forgotten emergency" – starkly demonstrates the fate of countries out of the political spotlight. Whether a particular humanitarian disaster qualifies as a "donor darling" or a "donor orphan" makes a huge difference. "Aid is a lottery," the UN's former top humanitarian official Jan Egeland stated. "You have twenty-five equally desperate communities taking part in this lottery for attention every week. Twenty-four lose and one wins."[28] A country or a region of central significance to major powers, however, has a far better chance of holding the winning ticket.

The R2P norm seeks to mitigate the overwhelming influence of state interests as the determining factor for robust involvement – it aims to be a principle rather than a tactic. As it advances, perhaps less pressing emergencies where states have a vested interest may not always trump more grave situations in which they do not.

CHAPTER SIX

What Next?

This final chapter explores the future of the humanitarian business by revisiting three plausible and possible solutions for improving the marketplace – for recipients as well as aid agencies. My proposed plan for the future revolves around acting on three preoccupations that have been central to my own work for some time. The first is the urgent need for what seems like the impossible task of consolidation or centralization of the atomized international humanitarian delivery system. The second consists of efforts to increase accountability and transparency across humanitarian suppliers. The third is the requirement for a more thoughtful humanitarianism, for more basic research as part of an effort to pursue humanitarian science (i.e., a field akin to military science) in order to learn lessons from previous successes and failures.

Consolidation Not Coordination

The lack of centralization is especially difficult for soldiers to understand because of their hierarchical structure and culture; but virtually anyone examining earlier descriptions in this book or other case materials would wonder about the number of humanitarian participants and the number of competing agendas and priorities. One could seemingly make a prima facie case that there are too many, but this obvious realization never gets beyond the discussion stage. One observer has

compared ongoing discussions about civil–military humanitarian cooperation to "marriage-counseling sessions for
civil–military peace operations. These counseling sessions,
like those for a committed, but troubled, marriage, continue
seemingly without end, with the same issues reappearing
time after time, unchanged."[1]

Afghanistan and Iraq substantiate that problems raising
their ugly heads from time to time in the 1990s were not
aberrations but early evidence of structural flaws that are now
glaring. "Coordination" may have been far-fetched but was at
least conceivable when only the UN system, the ICRC, and
a handful of NGOs were on the scene. Now, with low or no
barriers to entry and burgeoning numbers of humanitarian
players with resources to devote to a crisis, we also encounter other disparate actors (including outside militaries and
PMSCs) with an accompanying clash over values and turf. The
"atomization" of the humanitarian enterprise makes efforts to
coordinate inputs a fool's errand.

Arthur Helton – who was killed in Baghdad at UN headquarters while interviewing Sergio Vieira de Mello in August
2003 – earlier had asked a rhetorical question about aid in
Afghanistan that has even greater salience for Iraq: "How
coordinated can the effort be when donors will give money
through both multilateral and bilateral channels, international
organizations and NGOs will jockey for roles and money, and
relief work will run up against recovery and development
plans?"[2] The answer is evident in light of the collective action
problems outlined in previous chapters and so prominently
displayed in Afghanistan and Iraq: uncoordinated inputs
from the international humanitarian system result often in
counterproductive outputs and in any case less effective ones
than those who have invested in projects should expect.

In the absence of meaningful central authority – which
amounts to "coordination lite," which is rued by proponents

of centralization such as this author – some critics argue that all UN mechanisms constitute a hindrance rather than a help. Advocates for *laissez-faire* humanitarianism argue that a coherent strategy and a master design are unwise because they would work against the magic of the invisible hand in the marketplace in which individual agencies pursue independence and arrive at a sound division of labor. A subtler view is that creative chaos is better than botched efforts at coherence, which is all that is possible within the hopelessly decentralized UN and NGO systems. That is, the process is better self-regulated, however poorly coordinated, because it is preferable to have one layer of bureaucracy fewer rather than one more. As no one is really in charge and no one can be sure what will work, so the argument goes, why not make the best of it rather than merely adding a ceremonial layer?

My own view is quite different: the most obvious path to improved international responses would pass through a more top-down model with a better division of labor among the various political and military parts of the UN family and their most important operational humanitarian partners. It has been over two decades since the establishment of the DHA and over a decade since it changed names but not functions as OCHA. Not to put too fine a point on it, behind the mask of public eloquence is basic management ineptitude and a lack of courage to centralize. The DHA and OCHA have made little practical difference.

Given that there is also no single or simple way to measure needs across humanitarian crises or to assess the extent to which they are adequately or equitably satisfied by the growing number of agencies or their larger staffs, a number of efforts are underway to improve how humanitarians can more accurately measure needs and pool resources. Many rely on the UN's CAP as a proxy for the relationship between funding availability and requirements. The United Nations attempts to

spell out the funding requirements for priorities within countries in crisis and then calculates the resources committed for
those priorities. *GHA Report 2011* reports that in 2010 only
about 60 percent of CAP funding needs were met, "a significant drop" of over 10 percent from the preceding three years.[3]

Donors, moreover, have been channeling portions of their
multilateral funds through financing mechanisms such as
the UN's Central Emergency Response Fund (CERF), "which
helps to ensure more equitable funding between crises, and
the country-level pooled mechanisms, which are designed
to ensure that priority needs are met within specific crises."[4]
According to the *GHA Report 2011*, "some of the financing
reform efforts of the humanitarian agenda have borne fruit.
. . . [T]he pooled humanitarian funds of various kinds (emergency response funds (ERFs), [CERF], common humanitarian
funds (CHFs)) are facilitating an increase in the number of
donors contributing, without creating impossible coordination challenges."[5] All of CERF's funding is channeled to UN
agencies, while about half of the funds in the ERFs and CHFs
are given to UN organizations and international and local
NGOs capture the remainder. Although the total volume of
these funds increased from $583 million in 2006 to $853 million in 2010, the amount has not altered significantly since
the mechanisms were launched. The increased figure for
2010 reflects more funding for the natural disasters in Haiti
and Pakistan, and only represents about 8.4 percent of total
international aid.[6]

A parenthetical remark is in order concerning IDPs, whose
lot is especially problematic because no agency is responsible
and no legal statute guides state or agency behavior for what
are increasingly the main victims of wars.[7] Susan Martin
has made the counter-intuitive recommendation for a new
agency for IDPs because "[a]ccountability is the bottom line.
And no one is accountable."[8] Starting in 2005, the Inter-

agency Standing Committee (IASC) initiated the so-called "cluster" approach as the latest experiment in coordination, first to address the needs of IDPs, but then expanding more generally to other chronic and sudden-onset emergencies. It covers 11 thematic areas of humanitarian work (including, most importantly, water, sanitation, and hygiene; food and nutrition; shelter and camp management; and protection). In countries in crisis, clusters are led by one UN agency (usually the one dealing with the most acute perceived problem), sometimes with an NGO co-chair, which is supposed to act as a "provider of last resort" when gaps appear. One early (2007) authoritative assessment is underwhelming: "[T]he weight of evidence points to the conclusion that the costs and drawbacks of the new approach are exceeded by its benefits."[9] *The State of the World's Refugees 2012* points to the fact that the "cluster system has achieved a great deal since 2005 . . . [but] challenges remain."[10] This is UN-speak to reiterate the more direct evaluation cited above. Thus, hoping for the best from decentralization does not serve refugees either; creating yet another UN agency, for IDPs, certainly is undesirable. A single organization for war-torn societies is required.

We have stressed the extent to which the UN's default setting is coordination, the mere mention of which rightfully makes eyes glaze over because there is no power of the purse to compel tighter collaboration. Prospects for successful coordination of anything in this marketplace depend on getting the main UN operational agencies (UNHCR, UNICEF, UNDP, and WFP) and those outside the UN framework (ICRC and the International Organization for Migration and the largest international NGOs) to pull together. Wherever and whenever the United Nations orchestrates an overall humanitarian response, there is no structural explanation for coherent and effective efforts. When it happens, the explanation is good faith, personalities, luck, and serendipity. We should be able to do better.

It is time, certainly within the context of an international responsibility to protect civilians from mass atrocities, to consolidate the various moving parts of the core UN system and to concentrate subcontracts with a handful of the most professional international NGOs as part of a consolidated presence in war-torn societies. An increasingly small number of observers would dispute that the international humanitarian system would function better with fewer moving parts and more collective efforts instead of operating as a myriad of competitors in the unregulated free market.

To do that, donors should put their money where their mouths are; they should insist upon consolidation in the marketplace. As Linda Polman concluded, "[I]f the aid industry is left to control itself instead of being controlled, then reforms aren't going to happen any time soon."[11]

A small glimmer of hope appeared as Secretary-General Ban Ki-moon announced in January 2012 some ideas for a second term. Among them he called for convening "a world humanitarian summit" to discuss numerous issues, including "a shared international commitment to strengthen aid transparency" and "expanding support for pooled funding mechanisms."[12] Of course, this may be additional proof of UN smoke and mirrors, but it also could signal an opening for the kind of centralization and consolidation that is so desperately needed.

More Accountability and Transparency

Beyond a doubt there must be higher levels of accountability and transparency among actors in the marketplace. These include not only aid agencies, but also donors themselves and intervening militaries. The magnitude of actors and resources

circulating in the business requires robust and institutional-
ized accounting mechanisms to effectively disburse aid based
on need and to ensure its appropriate use.

Accountability can be identified as being in a position
to trace the spending of funds given by donors to subsidize
humanitarian action. And a key component of better knowledge and better accountability is bringing recipients into the
conversation, which is or should be a normative goal of outsiders lending helping hands. Janice Stein summarizes the
changes in administrative and accounting culture – driven
largely by an altered public administration agenda that seeks
to transplant the purported efficiencies of the for-profit sector
into the humanitarian marketplace – that have influenced the
reality of humanitarian action. She notes, "It is inconceivable
that, fifty years ago, humanitarian organizations operating in
war zones would spend any time at all considering 'outputs,'
'outcomes,' and 'benchmarking.'"[13]

The emphasis on the topic grew from the neoliberal ortho-
doxy of the 1980s, namely to reducing the role of the state and
handing over responsibility to commercial enterprises and,
for humanitarian delivery, to NGOs because of their perceived
efficiency. Until humanitarianism became a big business
in the 1990s and 2000s, however, there was little reason to
impose monitoring; it was simply easier to trust that NGOs
were doing their jobs. But this reality clearly changed, and as
Stein notes elsewhere, the preoccupation with accountability
indicated a maturing of humanitarianism; it was "growing
up."[14]

Despite improvements, we still lack longitudinal data
for basic categories such as expenditure, income, number
of organizations, and activities. James Fearon has made a
distinguished analytical career by exploring the shortcomings in various kinds of data. Explanations for the paucity of
data about the humanitarian business include the following:

agencies (as well as the military) are often not forthcoming; reporting periods vary; disbursements and commitments are not always distinguished; beneficiaries are hard to count; and, even among Western donor countries, common reporting requirements are absent. Moreover, prior to the 1980s, very few aid organizations documented changing mission statements; sources of income; how and where they spent their funds; and relationships with international and local partners. The accuracy of available data is questionable in light of too little standardization and too few common definitions.

Moreover, institutional memory within organizations is challenged by high staff turnover: for example, in recent years, 25 percent for the Red Cross Movement, 35 percent for CARE, and 50 percent for MSF. Many figures are anecdotal, but a recent comparison shows that the average duration of an expatriate mission for MSF is 5.2 months as compared to the ICRC's 10.1 months.[15]

Accountability necessarily involves power relationships: one party is accountable to another. The principal–agent relationship should be clear to anyone familiar with the adage about the piper, the payment, and the tune. The institutionalization and rationalization of accountability reflected the emergence and visibility of the humanitarian field per se, and also the increased pressure placed by those who paid the bills and who come under increasing pressure from parliamentarians and their constituents. Moreover, the financial and economic crisis that began in 2008 has made it necessary to justify expenditures that were once unquestioned.

Hence, it was necessary to rationalize and professionalize humanitarian action. As such, accountability is an uncomfortable topic within the humanitarian marketplace because it requires answering awkward questions. The responses differ for respondents, depending on the nature of their business and values; moreover, subcontractors (aid agencies) and contractors (donors) may disagree about the relative importance of various indicators.

To whom are aid agencies responsible – to their clients (or recipients) or to the sources of funds (parliaments, individuals, contractors)? For what are aid agencies responsible – for accurate accounting and cost-effective programs, on the one hand, or for the lives of those affected populations in their care, on the other hand? Are these targets related, or antithetical? How is performance monitored – by colleagues sharing the same values, by independent auditors, or through a survey among clients? What are the consequences of a failure to meet contractual obligations or expectations – a cut-back in funds or even termination of a contract, or rather a continuation because the trying circumstances surrounding the delivery of relief and protection make it easier to justify lower expectations?

While part of the drive toward accountability came from donors, those working on the ground or in headquarters for aid agencies also sought greater accountability to recipients. Measuring impact and determining the extent of success or failure are tough methodological tasks, especially in highly volatile and fluid emergency situations. What was once thought highly desirable and unproblematic has now become problematized. What was once received wisdom and taken for granted no longer is.

In the complex reality of humanitarian action, moreover, accountability to parliaments or individual supporters does not necessarily compute in a manner that the reader might logically expect. The fact that overheads are low or that central books are in balance communicates precious little about the quality of projects in far-away war zones. If what matters is that everything adds up on paper, accountability has very limited value-added. Moreover, the books and performance of even a major humanitarian organization tell us very little about its impact on and standing in the marketplace as a whole.

In that regard, real complications arise because of arbitrary, and short, periods for many contracts. This reality leads to "rubber accounting" in order to camouflage various costs. Because contracts with donors are almost always short term (three to six months is typical), organizational pressure exists to amortize high initial start-up costs. Additional contracts are necessary to recover the sunk costs of recruiting and hiring staff, renting and furnishing offices and lodgings, and importing vehicles, computers, and generators. Most projects thus are renewed because neither a contracting agency nor a contractor (the donor) has an interest in reporting unsuccessful or mediocre projects. Truth is seen as a danger because it could threaten an organization's survival if contracts were not renewed, and donors have no interest in being reprimanded for having contracted an unsuccessful contractor. Silence about errors serves everyone's interests, but it also means failing to learn lessons.

The preceding pages represent a modest step toward understanding and, hopefully, addressing a host of thorny challenges facing humanitarians. The next step would be to open a two-way street: that is, for agencies themselves to actively collaborate with scholars in framing research and making data and experiences available, what Janice Stein calls "joined-up thinking." However, she was also quick to point out that "accountability is no panacea."[16] Practitioners should help direct research toward issues, cases, and questions that have not been sufficiently investigated. Those aid workers toiling in the field, in particular, should be well placed to draw scholarly attention to neglected but necessary research that would help make the entire field more transparent and accountable. But enhancing accountability and transparency, however necessary, is a distant goal because of the ever-changing circumstances in which humanitarians operate.

A significant risk, however, may be that an obsession with narrow notions of accountability may force the very best agencies into risk-aversion, sapping their creative energies and commitments to the humanitarian cause. As the 2011 *World Development Report* noted, we should "expect a degree of failure in programs that require innovation and engagement with weak institutions in risky environments, and adapt accordingly."[17] Accountability that becomes routine and mechanical will consume precious resources and not benefit anyone, especially not the affected populations requiring assistance. As Stein tells us, such organizations can be "beautifully transparent and transparently mediocre."[18] Accountability can only work when it combines the highest standards from humanitarians about their own values with appropriate inputs from those who benefit as well as from those who provide the funding.

Aid agencies are not the only actors operating in the humanitarian arena that require enhanced accountability and transparency. Governments, as funders and operational humanitarian actors, do as well. The *GHA Report 2011*, however, noted that "the bases on which donors make their decisions are rarely made public. This lack of transparence as to who is funding what, and with what justification, creates a situation where a rational and proportional coverage of needs can only be received by chance rather than by the sum of informed individual donor choices."[19]

Military interveners must also be held accountable for their actions by the international community of states. In this context, "accountability" means the ability to ensure that a mission approved by the United Nations or a regional organization but then subcontracted to a powerful state or a coalition of the willing reflects collective interests and norms and not merely the national imperatives and preferences of the subcontractor. There are very limited means to ensure compliance by states generally, and ensuring account-ability clearly is more problematic when a powerful state seeks international approval of an intended or an ongoing military deployment. Nonetheless, intergovernmental decision-making organs (and specifically the UN Security Council) are in a position to refuse or delay approval and can demand that specific conditions pertaining to the character, size, timing, and goals of an operation be met before the potential subcontractor is given an international imprimatur. Ironically, UN approval became valuable to Washington and London in the aftermath of the 2003 Iraq war, given the enormous complexity and financial burden of post-conflict peacebuilding and reconstruction in that war-torn country. Ensuring accountability consists of three elements: effective mechanisms in the field; meaningful content to restrictions governing the behavior by the subcontractor; and costs associated with noncompliance.

In principle, major powers with a long democratic tradition are more likely to be embarrassed by criticisms of their behavior under a subcontract than are authoritarian governments. However, it is worth exploring when precisely the need for international sanctioning of actions by major powers affords the opportunity to require more of all states. Skeptics will no doubt argue that this is a slender reed on which to lean for a better system to maintain international peace and security; but it is at least preferable to gunboat diplomacy. Major powers inevitably flex their muscles – indeed, they "do not make great multilateralists"[20] – when their geopolitical interests are at stake; and they do not readily subject themselves to international monitoring and law. Although hardly a panacea, mapping steps toward more accountable subcontracting nonetheless would represent progress toward a more stable international order.[21]

More Reflection, Less Reaction

Aid agencies face a steep learning curve in the types of war zones discussed throughout this book. Responding effectively requires a new degree of knowledge and professionalism. There have been a number of international initiatives designed to improve the quality and reliability of humanitarian action by enhancing the training, preparation, and qualifications of aid workers – in short, "professionalizing" the sector in the same way that other associations of specialists such as accountants and physicians have done.[22] This progress has been substantial and important, but here we are interested in an entirely different level of openness to evidence-based action.

Responding from the heart remains a trademark, but effectiveness in today's crises requires at least an equal dose of well-informed tough-mindedness. Humanitarian personnel are specific targets of warring parties; insignia no longer afford protection; and emergency responses are but one element of a complex process of conflict resolution and social, economic, and political reconstruction. As such, reflection is more valuable than visceral reaction. Humanitarian impulses and goodwill are no longer adequate, if indeed they ever were. One common-sense piece of advice applies to the humanitarian marketplace: "look before you leap." But this also means turning another aphorism on its head, namely "don't just do something, stand there."

Why? The last two decades have witnessed examples of well-intentioned but ultimately counterproductive humanitarian action. The commitment to saving lives and relieving suffering can have the unintended consequences of fueling conflict, even of worsening some political crises and eroding the longer-term coping capacities of target societies. A skeptic or activist might also retort by pointing to the risks of "paralysis by analysis" – with research providing an excuse not to act

instead of how to act – but this cautionary note does not viti-
ate the overwhelming requirement for better data and more
informed decision-making.

The ongoing debate about calculating needs in war zones
also suggests that getting it wrong may have benefits for
resource mobilization. Among the most disputed were the
estimates that may have been inflated by two to three times by
the International Rescue Committee in the DRC. As Joshua
Goldstein notes, "The IRC authors themselves noted in 2006
that 'following the release of the 2000 survey results, total
humanitarian aid increased by over 500% between 2000 and
2001. The United States contribution alone increased by a
factor of almost twenty-six. It is probably fair to assert that the
mortality data played a significant role in increasing international assistance.'" However, there is a downside, as Goldstein
also calls to our attention, which is why getting a better handle
on humanitarian research is desirable: "On the one hand,
exaggerated figures apparently actually did draw the world's
attention to a forgotten conflict and thereby helped save lives.
On the other hand, making science serve political ends, even
desirable ones, usually does not end well."[23] Numbers, and
knowledge about them, are prerequisites for contemporary
mobilization to halt mass atrocities and deal with them. As
he has for many issues, David Rieff captured succinctly the
explanation for part of the knowledge gap, namely the "apocalypse mongering" that is part of the successful global business
model of "disaster hype."[24]

As the *GHA Report 2011* makes clear:

> In order for donors to make informed funding decisions to
> meet their commitments to fund in accordance with assessed
> needs, they need objective and comparable evidence that
> demonstrates the scale, severity and nature of humanitar-
> ian needs, and they also need to know what decisions others
> are making to ensure that resources are distributed equitably

across and within different crises. Yet serious deficiencies remain in both areas.[25]

The point here is that careful research could help bring substantially more benefits to victims. This recommendation may strike observers as a self-serving justification by someone whose professional career has been devoted to research. Nonetheless, the proposition is that more data-based social scientific reflection and less visceral reaction should help make the humanitarian business function better.[26]

The purpose of social science is to solve problems and improve society. At the turn of the seventeenth century, Francis Bacon specified the basics of induction; for him the purpose of scientific knowledge was to improve the common good, to which the Enlightenment was devoted. Michael Barnett's *Empire of Humanity* shows the prevalence of applying scientific knowledge to address social ills in the nineteenth century.[27] Rather than hoping for the magic of the invisible hand – which works no better in the humanitarian than other marketplaces – should we not determine how best to help and protect the most vulnerable individuals trapped in war zones?

The strength of social science lies in its ability to gather, organize, interpret, and disseminate evidence-based recommendations. When done properly, applied research should not only help the helpers but also improve the lives of those who are dependent temporarily on outside assistance. Social science specifically geared to humanitarianism is in its infancy, but important changes have taken place in the last two decades, at least partially because the shortcomings in delivery and protection have been recognized by humanitarians themselves. A growing openness to social science has appeared among aid personnel, a major cultural change that is reflected in a series of analytical efforts: the ICRC's *Avenir* initiative; the International Federation of Red Cross and Red

Crescent Societies' Sphere Project; the Active Learning for Accountability and Performance in Humanitarian Action (ALNAP); publications from the Humanitarianism & War Project, the Overseas Development Institute, and the Centre for Humanitarian Dialogue; and even in-depth research by individual agencies (following the example of Oxfam-UK, which has led the way with several paid staff working in a research and evaluation unit).

Aid agencies should be receptive to social science because it directly benefits the business of saving strangers. Humanitarians require discrete and usable knowledge that reformulates how to think about the marketplace and that better specifies cause–effect relationships. Such knowledge can be provided by social scientists, but too many aid agencies are poor at learning and adapting. The dominant culture is rapid reaction not reserved reflection. Larry Minear points out that "humanitarian organizations' adaptation to the new realities has been for the most part lethargic and phlegmatic."[28] To be blunt, humanitarians often are learning disabled because their culture is built on acting viscerally and not on processing information, correcting errors, and devising alternative strategies and tactics. Delivery and protection is the business of aid officials and properly preoccupies them. However, they should also recognize the value-added of social scientists. A partnership would benefit both, not to mention the denizens of war-torn societies.

The lack of learning does not necessarily mean a lack of lessons. Practitioners are catching on, but slowly. "[T]he profession is more self-conscious and sophisticated in its understanding of itself than ever before," Hugo Slim reminds us, but "the system is not very good at acting on what it knows." Social scientists can help provide knowledge, but practitioners must also engage in an ongoing struggle to consume and digest it. There is no quick fix here, only the long and arduous path of more deeply embedding the "culture of improvement," the norm of discovery and innovation.[29]

Donors must also overcome their reluctance – or even active hostility – to fund applied research. The trailblazing benefactor Andrew Carnegie practiced as well as preached "scientific philanthropy," bankrolling a variety of knowledge-based initiatives and institutions for the common good. We have noted the absence of longitudinal data, which makes it especially puzzling that donors are reluctant to finance research but simultaneously require more data to hold humanitarians accountable. Moreover, donors (especially parliaments) do not want to hear about failures, even ones from which better projects and programs emerge. There are many other problems facing someone seriously interested in research, including overcoming the reluctance of those responding to victims to give any kind of priority to gathering data. Humanitarian organizations themselves have no incentive to collect data unless it trumpets their successes, not exposes their flaws. There is no short-cut; more funds (or higher overheads, which amount to the same thing) and more dedicated personnel are required for data gathering, policy analysis, and strategic planning. Otherwise, we are condemned to have only partial stories that showcase horrifying tragedies and the need for more resources but ignore the hard truths so essential for learning.

While it may seem provocative, the proposal is to move toward the humanitarian equivalent of military science. For too long humanitarians have talked about becoming more professional but have been unwilling to accept the discipline and costs that necessarily would accompany such a decision. Too many projects and programs are driven by anecdote and angst, not data and detached deliberations. If effective humanitarian action is based on negotiating the best deal among the competing agendas of governments, insurgents, donors, and recipients (and none of these groups has a monolithic viewpoint), then better understanding is essential.

Humanitarians will undoubtedly take offense with my generalization, but they are in some ways less serious and less professional than their military counterparts. As the 2011 overview from the World Bank notes, the current system of institutions "is not well-adapted to today's reality of repeated cycles of instability and risks of criminal and political violence."[30] The military "culture" values learning, and supervisors invest substantial resources in the institutional infrastructure to assemble and act on lessons. Military academies are where previous and ongoing operations are analyzed, where new procedures are tried and tested, and where student-soldiers are obliged to learn about adopting best practices and adapting tactics to field specifics. Career development and promotions require regular time-off for further education and reflection before new assignments. Ongoing operations routinely have historians attached to them.

None of the above generalizations applies to the civilians operating in the marketplace. Unkind critics will certainly ridicule my praise for such military practices as reflecting institutional "fat" and overly generous budget allocations from parliaments. But it is more useful to view them as an essential cultural difference that humanitarians should emulate. Whereas practitioners have traditionally sought to distance themselves from scholars and policy analysts, the future bottom line for the humanitarian business would be improved by moving beyond the stereotype that presents practitioners as guardians and scholars or policy specialists as gadflies.

For generals as well as soldiers, the "fog of war" is vexing, but decision-makers at all levels in today's marketplace encounter the "fog of humanitarianism" and later the "fog of peacebuilding." The uncertainties that plague war and warriors are but one source of the dense cover that obscures the marketplace. Donor politics and traditional collective action problems further cloud policy and decision-making. Humanitarians are unable to completely lift the fog – and the winds of international politics are unlikely to disperse it – but its worst effects can be mitigated. Most critically, staff can be in a better position to navigate if they better understand the nature of change in war and humanitarianism and adjust their programming accordingly. What is needed is a strategic vision for humanitarianism – a framework that illuminates the nuts and bolts of tactical means–ends relationships in achieving the primary goal of saving lives.

In short, the future humanitarian marketplace requires more reflection and less reaction. To return to Francis Bacon, "*Scientia est potentas*" (knowledge is power). And that power should be harnessed for the good of vulnerable populations.

Conclusion: Toward Consequential Ethics

It is fitting to return to our point of departure. Humanitarianism is coming of age. It requires neither the denial of political and marketplace realities nor their uncritical embrace and worship. The *Human Security Report 2009/10* puts forward some encouraging data concerning the reduced risks of war seemingly resulting from the demise of colonialism and the Cold War along with the increasing levels of economic interdependence, the number of democracies, and evolving norms; and a similar conclusion was reached by Joshua Goldstein.[31] It is too early, however, for humanitarians to declare victory and celebrate. Number-crunchers are assessing the extent to which global data are better or worse than conventional wisdom would have it; but the economic, political, and moral challenges inherent in all of the crises of the past two decades have not become less acute. They continue in active war zones.

Humane values are best served by understanding and avoiding the possibilities for manipulation that are inherent not only in contemporary wars but also in the contemporary business model used by aid agencies in coming to the rescue of war-affected populations. Politics and business economics are best viewed as arenas that international pressure can make more hospitable and amenable to genuine humanitarian values and life-saving actions. At their best, they encompass a vision of human solidarity and embody a strategy that can render that solidarity a reality rather than an aspiration.

Modesty is a virtue for aid workers *and* social scientists. Many observers, and among them many of the most fervent and committed humanitarians whom I know, would have us believe in the humanitarian "imperative," which they define as the moral obligation to treat affected populations similarly and react to crises consistently wherever they may be. However, such a notion flies in the face of politics, which consists of drawing lines as well as weighing options and available resources in order to make tough decisions about doing the greatest good or the least harm, or even about what is imaginable let alone feasible.

A more accurate and laudable description of contemporary efforts to save strangers would be to pursue the humanitarian "impulse" – sometimes we can act and sometimes we cannot.[32] Humanitarian action is desirable, not obligatory. The humanitarian impulse is permissive; the humanitarian imperative would be peremptory. Setting aside for a moment the problems of measuring the costs and benefits, what remains clear is that the transformation of war and of the humanitarian marketplace requires the transformation of humanitarianism, altering the slope of the curves for demand and supply.

Nothing in these pages should even mildly hint at any disrespect for those who risk their lives to rescue and protect the vulnerable. There is no need to denigrate the heroic and unselfish acts of humanitarians or the value of compassion and charity. Yet a striking fact of contemporary international society is that the numbers of individuals and organizations acting to foster humanitarian norms and facilitate humanitarian action have risen dramatically, as has media attention. The paradox is that barbarism has increased apace and that the marketization of humanitarian action has led to rational and predictable, albeit often dysfunctional, responses by humanitarians to the incentives within the market in which they operate.

Addressing this puzzle necessitates hard-headed analysis and not the rigid application of moral absolutes. A more utilitarian tack specifies objectives and norms toward which to strive but without the illusion that success is guaranteed by the application of any formulas. Clashes among principles will continue – in the interpretation given to them by various individuals and agencies, in the importance of some relative to others, and in the extent to which a given principle or principles will prevail in particular circumstances.

Hopefully, the validity of a utilitarian approach should have been reinforced by these pages. Situational ethics are required. Moral ambiguity is no longer taboo among humanitarians. The articulation of principles remains important as a safeguard against the slippery slope of shameless and supine opportunism. But when principles bump into one another, compromise and tough trade-offs are inevitable. "All effective humanitarian action is based on negotiating compromises with the relevant political actors . . . and trying to reconcile competing agendas," David Rieff now argues. "For a humanitarian organization to believe and, far more importantly, to behave as if this were not the case is to court disaster."[33] Those who deviate from principles should be aware of the costs – and extenuating circumstances in all the cases in this book indicate why such deviations are unavoidable. Those with principles who are clear about the costs of deviating from them will be more successful in helping victims than those with no principles or with inflexible ones.

Frequently, the word "dilemma" is employed to describe painful decision-making, but the word "quandary" would be more apt. A dilemma involves two or more alternative courses of action with unintended, unavoidable, and *equally* undesirable consequences. If consequences are equally unpalatable, then remaining on the sidelines is a viable and moral option rather than entering the scrum on the field.

Humanitarians find themselves perplexed, or in a quandary, but they are not and should not be immobilized by contemporary wars. The key lies in making a good-faith effort to analyze the advantages and disadvantages of any military or civilian course of action and opt for what often amounts to the least-worst option. The calculus is agonizing but inescapable for those who work in the humanitarian business.

The situational morality championed by John Dewey emerges as a guide for humanitarians evaluating painful trade-offs. For too long, they have avoided or waffled on tough questions. Exempting the international humanitarian system from criticism and assuming that the results were inevitably worthwhile because the motives were noble is no longer an option. The following question should be continuously asked and answered: what is the balance when we weigh the positive versus the negative effects?

It thus is essential to move beyond a vulgar Kantianism and recognize the limits of "legalism," what Myron Wiener once called "monistic humanitarianism."[34] Decisions that are thoughtful and reflect realities on the ground are more appropriate than ones that automatically apply grand principles, for four reasons: there are often conflicting goals (among international refugee law, humanitarian law, and human rights law);

good intentions can have catastrophic consequences; there are alternative ways to achieve ends; and even if none of the choices is ideal, victims still require decisions about outside help. Analyses and not formulas are required. The task is thus to be flexible rather than to take preset criteria and apply them blindly.[35]

Many of the tactical as well as strategic decisions in the humanitarian marketplace – especially those involving the application of coercive military force – require selecting among terrible options. As the philosopher Thomas Nagel advises: "Given the limitations on human action, it is naïve to suppose that there is a solution to every moral problem."[36] Thus, action-oriented institutions and staff are required to contextualize their work and not blindly apply preconceived notions of what is right or wrong. Making decisions in war zones could benefit from the analogy to "clinical ethical review teams," whose members are on call to make painful decisions about life-and-death matters in hospitals. Although certain religious traditions claim that principles should be applied automatically, new technologies present unfamiliar situations in which principles clash and yet decisions are inescapable.

Tough love is necessary in today's hospitals and war zones. Finding solutions to challenges is emotionally wrenching but intellectually doable and operationally necessary. Doing nothing is not an option. Arthur Helton, who, as noted, died while conducting field research at UN headquarters in Baghdad in August 2003, decried "the price of indifference."[37] Or, as one advocate wrote about the rewards from making tough decisions, "nothing empowers people quite like their own survival."[38]

Indifference is not an option. If I were unkind, I would argue that those who cannot stand the heat generated by situational ethics should stay out of the humanitarian kitchen because it is not going to get cooler anytime soon. Understanding better the constraints on the humanitarian business and the limits of charity is a wise point of departure for the post-post-Cold War era.

Notes

ACKNOWLEDGMENTS

1 Larry Minear and Thomas G. Weiss, *Humanitarian Politics* (New York: Foreign Policy Association, 1995); and *Mercy under Fire: War and the Global Humanitarian Community* (Boulder, CO: Westview, 1995).

2 Thomas G. Weiss and Cindy Collins, *Humanitarian Challenges and Intervention*, 2nd edn (Boulder, CO: Westview, 2000).

3 International Commission on Intervention and State Sovereignty, *The Responsibility to Protect* (Ottawa: International Development Research Centre, 2001); and Thomas G. Weiss and Don Hubert, *The Responsibility to Protect: Research, Bibliography, Background* (Ottawa: International Development Research Centre, 2001).

4 See, for example, Gareth Evans, *The Responsibility to Protect: Ending Mass Atrocity Crimes Once and for All* (Washington, DC: Brookings Institution, 2008); Michael Ignatieff, *Human Rights as Politics and Idolatry*, edited and introduced by Amy Gutmann (Princeton, NJ: Princeton University Press, 2001); and Ramesh Thakur, *The United Nations, Peace and Security: From Collective Security to the Responsibility to Protect* (Cambridge: Cambridge University Press, 2006).

5 Peter J. Hoffman and Thomas G. Weiss, *Sword and Salve: Confronting New Wars and Humanitarian Crises* (Lanham, MD: Rowman & Littlefield, 2006).

6 Michael Barnett and Thomas G. Weiss, *Humanitarianism Contested: Where Angels Fear to Tread* (London: Routledge, 2011), and Michael Barnett and Thomas G. Weiss, eds., *Humanitarianism in Question: Politics, Power, Ethics* (Ithaca, NY: Cornell University Press, 2008).

7 Stephen Hopgood, *Keepers of the Flame: Understanding Amnesty International* (Ithaca, NY: Cornell University Press, 2006).
8 Hugo Slim, *Killing Civilians: Method, Madness and Morality in War* (New York: Columbia University Press, 2007).

INTRODUCTION

1 Harold Dwight Lasswell, *Politics: Who Gets What, When, How* (New York: Whittlesey House, 1936).
2 David Rieff, "Afterword," in *Humanitarian Negotiations Revealed: The MSF Experience*, ed. Claire Magone, Michael Neuman, and Fabrice Weissman (London: Hurst, 2012), p. 251.
3 Comments of an anonymous reviewer of the original proposal for this book.
4 Hugo Slim, "Marketing Humanitarian Space: Argument and Method in Humanitarian Persuasion," in *Essays in Humanitarian Action* (Oxford: Oxford Institute for Ethics, Law, and Armed Conflict, University of Oxford, 2012; Kindle edn).
5 James Rosenau, *Distant Proximities: Dynamics beyond Globalization* (Princeton, NJ: Princeton University Press, 2003).
6 António Guterres, "Foreword," in UNHCR, *The State of the World's Refugees 2012: In Search of Solidarity* (Oxford: Oxford University Press, 2012), p. x.
7 Naomi Klein, *The Shock Doctrine: The Rise of Disaster Capitalism* (New York: Metropolitan Books, 2007).
8 *Oxford English Dictionary* (Oxford: Oxford University Press, 1933).
9 Besides Jean Pictet, *The Fundamental Principles of the Red Cross* (Geneva: ICRC, 1979), see David P. Forsythe, *The Humanitarians: The International Committee of the Red Cross* (Cambridge: Cambridge University Press, 2005); and Thomas G. Weiss, "Principles, Politics, and Humanitarian Action," *Ethics & International Affairs* XIII (1999): 1–22.
10 Sarah Collinson and Samir Elhawary, *Humanitarian Space: A Review of Trends and Issues*, HPG Report 32 (London: Overseas Development Institute, 2012).
11 Adam Roberts, "The So-Called 'Right' of Humanitarian Intervention," in *Yearbook of International Humanitarian Law 2000*, Vol. 3 (The Hague: T.M.C. Asser, 2002), pp. 3–51.

12 Rory Stewart and Gerald Knaus, *Can Intervention Work?* (New York: Norton, 2011).
13 Donald C.F. Daniel and Bradd C. Hayes, *Coercive Inducement and the Containment of International Crises* (Washington, DC: US Institute of Peace, 1999).
14 Ian Brownlie, *International Law and the Use of Force by States* (Oxford: Clarendon Pess, 1996); and Martin Wight, *Power Politics* (New York: Penguin, 1979).

CHAPTER I   RESPONDING TO HUMANITARIAN DEMANDS

1 Michael Barnett, *Empire of Humanity: A History of Humanitarianism* (Ithaca, NY: Cornell University Press, 2011).
2 Craig Calhoun, "The Imperatives to Reduce Suffering: Charity, Progress, and Emergencies in the Field of Humanitarian Action," in *Humanitarianism in Question: Politics, Power, Ethics*, ed. Michael Barnett and Thomas G. Weiss (Ithaca, NY: Cornell University Press, 2008), pp. 73–97.
3 Karl Polanyi, *The Great Transformation: The Political and Economic Origins of Our Time* (Boston: Beacon Press, 1944).
4 Craig Calhoun, Frederick Cooper, and Kevin Moore, eds., *Lessons of Empire: Imperial Histories and American Power* (New York: New Press, 2006); Alice Conklin, *A Mission to Civilize: The Republican Idea of Empire in France and Africa, 1895–1930* (Stanford, CA: Stanford University Press, 1998); and Ann Stoler and Frederick Cooper, eds., *Tensions of Empire: Colonial Cultures in a Bourgeois World* (Berkeley: University of California Press, 1997).
5 Adam Hochshild, *King Leopold's Ghost: A Story of Greed, Terror, and Heroism in Colonial Africa* (New York: Mariner Books, 1999).
6 Lawrence Friedman and Mark McGarvie, eds., *Charity, Philanthropy, and Civility in American History* (Cambridge: Cambridge University Press, 2003).
7 See François Bugnion, *The International Committee of the Red Cross and the Protection of War Victims* (Geneva: ICRC, 2003), Chapter 2.
8 Rachel McCleary, *Global Compassion: Private Voluntary Organizations and US Foreign Policy since 1939* (Oxford: Oxford University Press, 2009), pp. 16 and 3–35.

9   These figures are drawn from a 2003 OCHA roster (which no longer is updated).

10 Linda Polman, *The Crisis Caravan: What's Wrong with Humanitarian Aid?* (New York: Henry Holt, 2010), p. 10.

11 John Arquilla and David Ronfeldt, *Swarming and the Future of Conflict* (Washington, DC: Rand Corporation, 2000).

12 McCleary, *Global Compassion*, p. 16 and especially pp. 3–35.

13 Abby Stoddard, Adele Harmer, and Katherine Haver, *Providing Aid in Insecure Environments: Trends in Policy and Operations*, HPG Report 23 (London: Overseas Development Institute, 2006).

14 Peter Walker and Catherine Russ, *Professionalizing the Humanitarian Sector: A Scoping Study*, report commissioned by Enhancing Learning & Research for Humanitarian Assistance, April 2010, pp. 11–12.

15 See Hugo Slim, "Protecting Civilians: Putting the Individual at the Humanitarian Centre," in *The Humanitarian Decade: Challenges for Humanitarian Assistance in the Last Decade and into the Future*, Vol. 2, ed. OCHA (New York: UN, 2004), pp. 154–69.

16 Mark Duffield, *Global Governance and the New Wars: The Merging of Development and Security* (New York: Zed, 2001), p. 12. See also Philip White, "Complex Political Emergencies – Grasping Contexts, Seizing Opportunities," *Disasters* 24, no. 4 (2000): 288–90.

17 Michael Howard, "The Historical Development of the UN's Role in International Security," in *United Nations: Divided World*, ed. Adam Roberts and Benedict Kingsbury, 2nd edn (Oxford: Oxford University Press, 1993), pp. 69–70.

18 Hugo Slim, *Essays in Humanitarian Action* (Oxford: Oxford Institute of Ethics, Law and Armed Conflict, 2012).

19 Thomas G. Weiss, *Humanitarian Intervention: Ideas in Action*, 2nd edn (Cambridge: Polity Press, 2012).

20 Christine Bourloyannis, "The Security Council of the United Nations and the Implementation of International Humanitarian Law," *Denver Journal of International Law and Policy* 20, no. 3 (1993): 43.

21 T.A. van Baarda, "The Involvement of the Security Council in Maintaining International Law," *Netherlands Quarterly of Human Rights* 12, no. 1 (1994): 140.

22 Kofi A. Annan, *The Question of Intervention: Statements by the Secretary-General* (New York: UN, 1999).

23 International Commission on Intervention and State Sovereignty, *The Responsibility to Protect* (Ottawa: International Development Research Centre, 2001); and Thomas G. Weiss and Don Hubert, *The Responsibility to Protect: Research, Bibliography, Background* (Ottawa: International Development Research Centre, 2001).

24 Benedict Anderson, *Imagined Communities* (London: Verso, 1983).

25 Michael Klein, *The Market for Aid* (Washington, DC: World Bank, 2005).

26 This section draws on Thomas G. Weiss, *Military–Civilian Interactions: Humanitarian Crises and the Responsibility to Protect*, 2nd edn (Lanham, MD: Rowman & Littlefield, 2005), pp. 1–26.

27 Peter Willetts, *Non-Governmental Organizations in World Politics* (London: Routledge, 2011).

28 Alexander Cooley and James Ron, "The NGO Scramble: Organizational Insecurity and the Political Economy of Transnational Action," *International Security* 27, no. 1 (2002): 5–39; and Dorothea Hilhorst, "Being Good at Doing Good? Quality and Accountability of Humanitarian NGOs," *Disasters* 26, no. 3 (2002): 193–212.

29 See David P. Forsythe and Barbara Ann Rieffer-Flanagan, *The International Committee of the Red Cross* (London: Routledge, 2007).

30 Michael Ignatieff, *The Warrior's Honor: Ethnic War and the Modern Conscience* (New York: Holt, 1997). David Forsythe's classic book, *Humanitarian Politics: The International Committee of the Red Cross* (Baltimore, MD: Johns Hopkins University Press, 1977), argued that the ICRC was engaged politically, which is updated in his *The Humanitarians*. See also John F. Hutchinson, *Champions of Charity: War and the Rise of the Red Cross* (Boulder, CO: Westview, 1996).

31 Thomas G. Weiss, David P. Forsythe, Roger A. Coate, and Kelly-Kate Pease, *The United Nations and Changing World Politics*, 6th edn (Boulder, CO: Westview, 2010).

32 Gil Loescher, Alexander Betts, and James Milner, *The UNHCR*, 2nd edn (London: Routledge, 2011); Arthur Helton, *The Price of Indifference: Refugees and Humanitarian Action in the New Century*

(Oxford: Oxford University Press, 2002); Stephen John Stedman and Fred Tanner, eds., *Refugee Manipulation: War, Politics, and Human Misery* (Washington, DC: Brookings Institution, 2003); and UNHCR, *The State of the World's Refugees 2000: Fifty Years of Humanitarian Action* (Oxford: Oxford University Press, 2000).

33 Yves Beigbeder, *The New Challenges for UNICEF: Children, Women and Human Rights* (New York: Palgrave, 2001); and Richard Jolly, *UNICEF* (London: Routledge, 2012).

34 See John D. Shaw, *Global Food and Agricultural Institutions* (London: Routledge, 2009) and *The UN World Food Programme and the Development of Food Aid* (Basingstoke: Palgrave, 2001).

35 Stephen Browne, *The UN Development Programme and System* (London: Routledge, 2011).

36 Larry Minear, *The Humanitarian Enterprise: Dilemmas and Discoveries* (Bloomfield, CT: Kumarian, 2002); and Jonathan Moore, *The UN and Complex Emergencies* (Geneva: UN Research Institute for Social Development, 1996).

37 For a historical treatment of disparities in international peace operations in Africa, see Adekeye Adebajo, *UN Peacekeeping in Africa: From the Suez Crisis to the Sudan Conflicts* (Boulder, CO: Lynne Rienner Publishers, 2011).

38 Frederick C. Cuny, "Dilemmas of Military Involvement in Humanitarian Relief," in *Soldiers, Peacekeepers, and Disasters*, ed. Leon Gordenker and Thomas G. Weiss (London: Macmillan, 1991), p. 54.

39 Adam Roberts, "Humanitarian War: Military Intervention and Human Rights," *International Affairs* 69 (1993): 429–49; and David Rieff, *A Bed for the Night: Humanitarianism in Crisis* (New York: Simon & Schuster, 2002).

40 The most relevant treatment of this topic is Peter J. Hoffman, *The New Politics of Protecting Humanitarian Space: A Private Security Revolution in Humanitarian Affairs?*, unpublished Ph.D. dissertation, The Graduate Center, The City University of New York, 2012.

41 Available at: www.icrc.org/ihl.nsf/full/470?opendocument (accessed July 16, 2012).

42 Adopted in 1977 by the Organization of African Unity; entered into force in 1985, available at: www.icrc.org/ihl.nsf/0/5e41dd4e 2010663fc125641e0052c016?OpenDocument (accessed July 13, 2012).

43 Adopted by the General Assembly in 1989, available at: www.
    un.org/documents/ga/res/44/a44r034.htm (accessed July 13,
    2012).
44 See: www.ohchr.org/EN/Issues/Mercenaries/WGMercenaries/
    Pages/WGMercenariesIndex.aspx (accessed July 16, 2012).
45 Michael T. Klare, *Resource Wars: The New Landscape of Global
    Conflict* (New York: Henry Holt, 2002), especially pp. 190–212.
46 See Doug Brooks, "Messiahs or Mercenaries? The Future
    of International Private Military Services," *International
    Peacekeeping* 7, no. 4 (2000): 129–44; Christopher Spearin,
    "Private Security Companies and Humanitarians: A Corporate
    Solution to Securing Humanitarian Spaces?" *International
    Peacekeeping* 8, no. 1 (2001): 20–43; and Damian Lilly, Tony
    Vaux, Chris Seiple, Greg Nakano, and Koenraad Van Brabant,
    *Humanitarian Action and Private Security Companies: Opening the
    Debate* (London: International Alert, May 2002).
47 Kofi Annan, *Thirty-fifth Annual Ditchley Foundation Lecture*,
    United Nations press release SG/SM/6613, 26 June 1998. See
    Deborah D. Avant, *The Market for Force: The Consequences of
    Privatizing Security* (Cambridge: Cambridge University Press,
    2005), pp. 193–7.
48 Michael Bryans, Bruce D. Jones, and Janice Gross Stein, "Mean
    Times: Humanitarian Action in Complex Political Emergencies
    – Stark Choices, Cruel Dilemmas," *Coming to Terms* 1, no. 3
    (1999), available at: www.grandslacs.net/doc/1141.pdf (accessed
    July 16, 2012).
49 Peter W. Singer, *Corporate Warriors: The Rise of the Privatized
    Military Industry* (Ithaca, NY: Cornell University Press, 2003),
    p. 82.
50 Duffield, *Global Governance and the New Wars*; Alex de Waal,
    Famine Crimes: Politics and the Disaster Relief Industry in Africa
    (Oxford: James Currey, 1997); and Michael Maren, *The Road to
    Hell: The Ravaging Effects of Foreign Aid and International Charity*
    (New York: Free Press, 1997).
51 Joanna Macrae, "Defining the Boundaries: International Security
    and Humanitarian Engagement in the Post-Cold War World,"
    in *The Humanitarian Decade: Challenges for Humanitarian
    Assistance in the Last Decade and into the Future*, Vol. 2, ed.
    OCHA (New York: UN, 2004), p. 116.
52 Rony Brauman and Pierre Salignon, "Iraq: In Search of a

'Humanitarian Crisis,'" in *In the Shadow of "Just Wars": Violence, Politics, and Humanitarian Action*, ed. Fabrice Weissman (Ithaca, NY: Cornell University Press, 2004), p. 271.

53 Greg Hansen, *Perceptions of Humanitarianism in Iraq*, Briefing Paper 6, no. 1 (New York: NGO Coordinating Committee on Iraq, 2008).

54 Ian Smillie and Larry Minear, *The Charity of Nations: Humanitarian Action in a Calculating World* (Bloomfield, CT: Kumarian, 2004), p. 18.

55 Carlotta Gall and Amy Waldman, "Under Siege in Afghanistan, Aid Groups Say Their Effort Is Being Criticized Unfairly," *New York Times*, December 19, 2004.

56 Global Witness, *Faced with a Gun, What Can You Do? War and the Militarization of Mining in Eastern Congo*, December 5, 2009, available at: www.globalwitness.org/library/global-witness-report-faced-gun-what-can-you-do (accessed July 13, 2012).

57 Ignatieff, *The Warrior's Honor*; and Stephen Hopgood, *Keepers of the Flame: Understanding Amnesty International* (Ithaca, NY: Cornell University Press, 2006).

58 Stephen Hopgood, "Saying 'No' to Wal-Mart? Money and Morality in Professional Humanitarianism," in *Humanitarianism in Question*, ed. Barnett and Weiss, pp. 98–123.

59 Quoted by Naomi Klein, "Disaster Capitalism: The New Economy of Catastrophe," *Harper's Magazine* (October 2007): 51.

60 Hopgood, "Saying 'No' to Wal-Mart?," p. 123.

61 Nik Gowing, *Media Coverage: Help or Hindrance in Conflict Prevention?* (New York: Carnegie Commission on the Prevention of Deadly Conflict, 1997); Warren Strobel, *Late Breaking Foreign Policy: The News Media's Influence on Peace Operations* (Washington, DC: United States Institute for Peace Press, 1997); and Larry Minear, Colin Scott, and Thomas G. Weiss, *The News Media, Civil War, and Humanitarian Action* (Boulder, CO: Lynne Rienner Publishers, 1996).

62 William Shawcross, *The Quality of Mercy* (New York: Simon & Schuster, 1984).

63 W. Joseph Campbell, "You Furnish the Legend, I'll Furnish the Quote," *American Journalism Review* (December 2001), available at: www.ajr.org/Article.asp?id=2429 (accessed July 1, 2012).

64 Andrew S. Natsios, *US Foreign Policy and the Four Horsemen*

of the Apocalypse: Humanitarian Relief in Complex Emergencies (Westport, CT: Praeger, 1997), p. 124.

65 International Federation of Red Cross and Red Crescent Societies, *World Disasters Report 2003: Focus on Ethics in Aid* (Bloomfield, CT: Kumarian, 2003), pp. 19–22.

66 Robert D. Kaplan, *The Coming Anarchy: Shattering the Dreams of the Post-Cold War World* (New York: Random House, 2000); and Samuel Huntington, *The Clash of Civilizations and the Remaking of World Order* (New York: Simon & Schuster, 1996).

67 Michael Ignatieff, "The Stories We Tell: Television and Humanitarian Aid," in *Hard Choices: Moral Dilemmas in Humanitarian Intervention*, ed. Jonathan Moore (Lanham, MD: Rowman & Littlefield, 1998), pp. 298, 301.

68 Nik Gowing, "The Upside and Downside of New Media Noise in Humanitarian Emergencies," in *The Humanitarian Decade: Challenges for Humanitarian Assistance in the Last Decade and into the Future*, Vol. 2, ed. OCHA (New York: UN, 2004), p. 216.

69 John C. Hammock and Joel C. Charny, "Emergency Responses as Morality Play," in *From Massacres to Genocide: The Media, Public Policy, and Humanitarian Crises*, ed. Robert I. Rotberg and Thomas G. Weiss (Washington, DC: Brookings Institution, 1996), pp. 115–35.

CHAPTER 2 THE CONTEMPORARY LANDSCAPE:
NEED AND GREED

1 This chapter draws upon Thomas G. Weiss, *Humanitarian Intervention: Ideas in Action*, 2nd edn (Cambridge: Polity Press, 2012), Chapter 3.

2 Mary Kaldor, *New and Old Wars: Organized Violence in a Global Era* (Stanford, CA: Stanford University Press, 1999); Mark Duffield, *Global Governance and the New Wars: The Merging of Development and Security* (London: Zed, 2001); and Robert Kaplan, *The Coming Anarchy: Shattering the Dreams of the Post-Cold War* (New York: Random House, 2000).

3 Edward Newman, "The 'New Wars' Debate: A Historical Perspective Is Needed," *Security Dialogue* 35, no. 2 (2004): 173–89; Stathis N. Kalyvas, "'New' and 'Old' Civil Wars: A Valid Distinction?" *World Politics* 54 (October 2001): 99–118.

4 See Bertrand Badie, *The Imported State: The Westernization of the Political Order* (Stanford, CA: Stanford University Press, 2000).

5 John Gerard Ruggie, "Territoriality and Beyond: Problematizing Modernity in International Relations," *International Organization* 47 (Winter 1993): 165.

6 Janice E. Thomson, "State Sovereignty in International Relations: Bridging the Gap between Theory and Empirical Research," *International Studies Quarterly* 39 (June 1995): 213–33, and Kalevi J. Holsti, *The State, War, and the State of War* (Cambridge: Cambridge University Press, 1996), pp. 82–98.

7 Samuel Huntington, *Political Order in Changing Societies* (New Haven, CT: Yale University Press, 1968); and Joel Migdal, *Strong States, Weak Societies: State–Society Relations and State Capabilities in the Third World* (Princeton, NJ: Princeton University Press, 1988).

8 Gerald B. Helman and Steven R. Ratner, "Saving Failed States," *Foreign Policy*, no. 89 (Winter 1992–3): 3–20.

9 See Robert I. Rotberg, "Failed States in a World of Terror," *Foreign Affairs* 81, no. 4 (2002): 127–40.

10 Hedley Bull, *The Anarchical Society: A Study of Order in World Politics* (New York: Columbia University Press, 1977).

11 Jessica Matthews, "Power Shift," *Foreign Affairs* 76 (January/February 1997): 61.

12 Mohammed Ayoob, *The Third World Security Predicament: State Making, Regional Conflict, and the International System* (Boulder, CO: Lynne Rienner Publishers, 1995).

13 Kalevi J. Holsti, *Taming the Sovereigns: Institutional Change in International Politics* (Cambridge: Cambridge University Press, 2004), p. 318.

14 James N. Rosenau, *Turbulence in World Politics* (Princeton, NJ: Princeton University Press, 1990).

15 Stephen J. Stedman and Fred Tanner, eds., *Refugee Manipulation: War, Politics, and the Abuse of Human Suffering* (Washington, DC: Brookings Institution, 2003), p. 14.

16 Beatrice Hibou, "The 'Social Capital' of the State as an Agent of Deception," in *The Criminalization of the State in Africa*, ed. Jean-François Bayart, Stephen Ellis, and Beatrice Hibou (Bloomington: Indiana University Press, 1999), p. 102.

17 Bernard Frahi, "Organized Crime and Conflict – Interaction and Policy Implications," in *Organized Crime as an Obstacle*

to *Successful Peacebuilding: Lessons Learned from the Balkans, Afghanistan, and West Africa – 7th International Berlin Workshop*, ed. Alexander Austin, Tobias von Gienanth, and Wibke Hansen (Berlin: Zentrum für Internationale Friedenseinsätze, 2003), pp. 35–6.

18 This definition is adapted from Stephen Stedman, who coined the term, defining it as: "leaders and parties who believe that peace emerging from negotiations threatens their power, worldview, and interests, and use violence to attempt to undermine efforts to achieve it." Stephen John Stedman, "Spoiler Problems in Peace Processes," *International Security* 22, no. 2 (1997): 5.

19 P.W. Singer, *Corporate Warriors: The Rise of the Privatized Military Industry* (Ithaca, NY: Cornell University Press, 2003), pp. 45–7; and Robert Mandel, *Armies without States: The Privatization of Security* (Boulder, CO: Lynne Rienner Publishers, 2002), pp. 9–10.

20 David Keen, "Incentives and Disincentives for Violence," in *Greed and Grievance: Economic Agendas in Civil War*, ed. Mats Berdal and David Malone (Boulder, CO: Lynne Reinner Publishers, 2000), p. 27, emphasis in original.

21 In addition to ibid., pp. 24–7 and 29–31, see William Reno, "Shadow States and the Political Economy of Civil War," in *Greed and Grievance*, ed. Berdal and Malone, pp. 44–5. Also see Halvor Mehlum, Karl Ove Moene, and Ragnar Torvik, "Plunder & Protection, Inc.," *Journal of Peace Research* 39, no. 4 (2002): 447–59.

22 Mary B. Anderson, *Do No Harm: How Aid Can Support Peace – or War* (Boulder, CO: Lynne Rienner Publishers, 1999), p. 46; Matthew LeRiche, "Unintended Alliance: The Co-option of Humanitarian Aid in Conflicts," *Parameters* (Spring 2004): 104–20; and David Keen, *The Benefits of Famine and Relief in Southwestern Sudan, 1983–1989* (Princeton, NJ: Princeton University Press, 1994).

23 Daniel Unger, "Ain't Enough Blanket: International Humanitarian Assistance and Cambodian Political Resistance," in *Refugee Manipulation: War, Politics, and the Abuse of Human Suffering*, ed. Stephen J. Stedman and Fred Tanner (Washington, DC: Brookings Institution, 2003), pp. 17–56; Frédéric Grare, "The Geopolitics of Afghan Refugees in Pakistan," in *Refugee*

Manipulation: War, Politics, and the Abuse of Human Suffering,
ed. Stephen J. Stedman and Fred Tanner (Washington,
DC: Brookings Institution, 2003), pp. 57–94; and LeRiche,
"Unintended Alliance," pp. 107, 115.

24 Human Rights Watch, "Civilian Devastation – Abuses by All
Parties in the War in Southern Sudan," 1993, available at: www.
hrw.org/reports/1993/sudan (accessed Juy 17, 2012).

25 Hugo Slim, *Killing Civilians: Methods, Madness and Morality in
War* (New York: Columbia University Press, 2007).

26 Alexander B. Downes, "Desperate Times, Desperate Measures:
The Causes of Civilian Victimization in War," *International
Security* 30, no. 4 (2006): 152.

27 See "Special Feature: The Great War in Numbers," available at:
www.worldwar1.com/sfnum.htm (accessed July 17, 2012).

28 Carnegie Commission on Preventing Deadly Conflict, *Preventing
Deadly Conflict: Final Report* (Washington, DC: Carnegie
Commission on Preventing Deadly Conflict, 1998), p. 11.

29 Kaldor, *New and Old Wars*, pp. 8, 100.

30 Holsti, *Taming the Sovereigns*, pp. 284–5.

31 Virgil Hawkins, "The Price of Inaction: The Media and
Humanitarian Intervention," *Journal of Humanitarian Assistance*,
May 25, 2001, available at: sites.tufts.edu/jha/archives/1504
(accessed July 17, 2012).

32 Adam Roberts, "Lives and Statistics: Are 90% of War Victims
Civilians?" *Survival* 52, no.3 (2010): 115–36; Human Security
Report Project, *Human Security Report 2009/2010: The Causes of
Peace and the Shrinking Costs of War* (Oxford: Oxford University
Press, 2011); Steven Pinker, *The Better Angels of Our Nature:
Why Violence Has Declined* (New York: Viking, 2011); and Joshua
S. Goldstein, *Winning the War on War: The Decline of Armed
Conflict Worldwide* (New York: Dutton, 2011).

33 See World Food Programme website at: www.wfp.org/hunger/
causes (accessed July 17, 2012).

34 UNHCR, *The State of the World's Refugees 2012: In Search of
Solidarity* (Oxford: Oxford University Press, 2012), p. 21.

35 See Joanna Macrae, ed., *The New Humanitarianisms: A Review
of Trends in Global Humanitarian Action* (London: Overseas
Development Institute, 2002); and Thomas G. Weiss,
"Principles, Politics, and Humanitarian Action," *Ethics &
International Affairs* XIII (1999): 1–22.

36 Michael Barnett, "Humanitarianism Transformed," *Perspectives on Politics* 3, no. 4 (2005): 723–41.
37 B.S. Chimni, "The Meaning of Words and the Role of UNHCR in Voluntary Repatriation," *International Journal of Refugee Law* 5, no. 3 (1993): 444; and Gervase Coles, *Solutions to the Problems of Refugees and Protection of Refugees: A Background Study* (Geneva: UNHCR, 1989), p. 203.
38 This phrase was popularized by Roberta Cohen and Francis M. Deng in *Masses in Flight: The Global Crisis of Internal Displacement* (Washington, DC: Brookings Institution, 1998), p. 10; and "Exodus within Borders," *Foreign Affairs* 77, no. 4 (1998): 15.
39 Antonio Donini, *The Future of Humanitarian Action: Implications of Iraq and Other Recent Crises* (Medford, MA: Tufts University, 2004); and Fiona Fox, "New Humanitarianism: Does It Provide a Moral Banner for the 21st Century?" *Disasters* 25, no. 4 (2001): 275–89.
40 Michael Bryans, Bruce D. Jones, and Janice Gross Stein, "Mean Times: Humanitarian Action in Complex Political Emergencies – Stark Choices, Cruel Dilemmas," *Coming to Terms* 1, no. 3 (1999): 9–10, available at: www.grandslacs.net/doc/1141.pdf (accessed July 16, 2012).
41 Bruce M. Oswald, "The Creation and Control of Places of Protection during United Nations Peace Operations," *International Review of the Red Cross* 83, no. 844 (December 2001): 1013.
42 David Rieff, "Afterword," in *Humanitarian Negotiations Revealed: The MSF Experience*, ed. Claire Magone, Michael Neuman, and Fabrice Weissman (London: Hurst, 2012), p. 254.
43 Michael Barnett and Martha Finnemore, *Rules for the World: International Organizations in Global Order* (Ithaca, NY: Cornell University Press, 2004), pp. 73–120. For UNHCR's views on repatriation see *State of the World's Refugees: Fifty Years of Humanitarian Action* (New York: Oxford University Press, 2000), pp. 155–83.
44 Rama Mani and Thomas G. Weiss, eds., *Responsibility to Protect: Cultural Perspectives in the Global South* (London: Routledge, 2011).
45 Global Humanitarian Assistance, *GHA Report 2011* (Wells, UK: Development Initiatives, 2011), pp. 24, 55, available at: www.

globalhumanitarianassistance.org/reports (accessed July 18, 2012).

46 See Development Assistance Committee, *Development Cooperation Report 2000* (Paris: Organization for Economic Co-operation and Development, 2001), pp. 180–1.

47 Global Humanitarian Assistance, *GHA Report 2011*.

48 Ibid., p. 6.

49 António Guterres, "Foreword," in UNHCR, *The State of the World's Refugees 2012: In Search of Solidarity* (Oxford: Oxford University Press, 2012), p. x.

50 Michael Barnett and Janice Gross Stein, "Introduction: The Secularization and Sanctification of Humanitarianism," in *Sacred Aid: Faith and Humanitarianism*, ed. Michael Barnett and Janice Gross Stein (Oxford: Oxford University Press, 2012), p. 7.

51 Global Humanitarian Assistance, *GHA Report 2009* (Wells, UK: Development Initiatives, 2009), p. 4, available at: www.globalhumanitarianassistance.org/reports (accessed July 18, 2012).

52 Joanna Macrae, Sarah Collinson, Margue Buchanan-Smith, Nicola Reindorp, Anna Schmidt, Tasneem Mowjee, and Adele Harmer, *Uncertain Power: The Changing Role of Official Donors in Humanitarian Action*, HPG Report 12 (London: Overseas Development Institute, 2002), p. 15; and Judith Randel and Tony German, "Trends in Financing of Humanitarian Assistance," in *The New Humanitarianisms: A Review of Trends in Global Humanitarian Action*, ed. Joanna Macrae (London: Overseas Development Institute, 2002), pp. 19–28.

53 Global Humanitarian Assistance, *GHA Report 2003* (Wells, UK: Development Initiatives, 2003), pp. 1, 14–15, available at: www.globalhumanitarianassistance.org/reports (accessed July 18, 2012).

54 Global Humanitarian Assistance, *GHA Report 2011*, p. 18.

55 See Abby Stoddard, "Dommage collatéral: contre-insurrection internationalisée et ses consequences néfastes sur l'action humanitaire," in *Dans l'oeil des autres: perception de l'action humanitaire de MSF*, ed. Caroline Abu-Sada (Lausanne: Éditions Antipodes, 2011).

56 Adele Harmer and Ellen Martin, *Diversity in Donorship: Field Lessons*, HPG Report 30 (London: Overseas Development Institute, 2010), p. 1.

57 Global Humanitarian Assistance, *GHA Report 2011*, p. 17.
58 Ibid., p. 13.
59 Relief Web, "International: Changes in Aid Pose Challenges," April 15, 2010, available at: www.reliefweb.int/rw/rwb.nsf/ db900sid/VDUX-84JSAS?OpenDocument (accessed July 17, 2012).
60 Global Humanitarian Assistance, *GHA Report 2011*, p. 17.
61 Adele Harmer and Lin Cotterrell, *Diversity in Donorship: The Changing Landscape of Official Humanitarian Aid*, HPG report 20 (London: Overseas Devvelopment Institute, 2005), quotes from pp. 3 and 6, statistics from pp. 7 and 5.
62 Global Humanitarian Assistance, *GHA Report 2011*.
63 Hugo Slim, "Global Welfare A Realistic Expectation for the International Humanitarian System?" *ALNAP Review of Humanitarian Action in 2005: Evaluation Utilisation* (December 2006), p. 21.
64 Chandra Lekha Sriram, John C. King, Julie A. Mertus, Olga Martin-Ortega, and Johanna Herman, eds., *Surviving Field Research: Working in Violent and Difficult Situations* (London: Routledge, 2009).
65 Cate Buchanan and Robert Muggah, *No Relief: Surveying the Effects of Gun Violence on Humanitarian and Development Personnel* (Geneva: Centre for Humanitarian Dialogue, 2005), pp. 7, 9.
66 Carlotta Gall and Amy Waldman, "Under Siege in Afghanistan, Aid Groups Say Their Effort Is Being Criticized Unfairly," *New York Times*, December 19, 2004.
67 OCHA, *To Stay and Deliver: Good Practice for Humanitarians in Complex Security Environments* (New York: OCHA, 2011).
68 Independent Panel on Safety and Security of United Nations Personnel and Premises, *Towards a Culture of Security and Accountability*, UN document dated 30 June 2008, available at: www.humansecuritygateway.com/showRecord. php?RecordId=25173 (accessed July 17, 2012).
69 Pierre-Michel Fontaine, "New Threats against Humanitarian Workers," *Refugee Survey Quarterly* 23, no. 4 (2004): 168.
70 Jan Egeland, *A Billion Lives: An Eyewitness Report from the Frontlines of Humanity* (New York: Simon & Schuster, 2008), p. 8.
71 "More Dangerous to Work than Ever," *The Economist*, 20 November 2004: 49.

72 Abby Stoddard, Adele Harmer, and Katherine Haver, *Providing Aid in Insecure Environments: Trends in Policy and Operations*, HPG Report 23 (London: Overseas Development Institute, 2006), quote and figures from pp. 1, 13.

73 Abby Stoddard, Adele Harmer, and and Katherine Haver, *Aid Worker Security Report 2011: Spotlight on Security for National Aid Workers* (London: Overseas Development Institute, 2006).

74 Committee to Protect Journalists, "Iraq: Journalists in Danger," available at: www.cpj.org/Briefings/Iraq/Iraq_danger.html (accessed July 17, 2012).

75 Michael Astor, "Iraq's Heavy Journalist Death Toll Keeps Climbing," Huffpost Media, September 7, 2010, available at: www.huffingtonpost.com/2010/09/07/iraqs-heavy-journalist-de_n_708299.html (accessed July 17, 2012).

76 Stoddard et al., *Providing Aid in Insecure Environments*, p. 39.

77 Linda Polman, *The Crisis Caravan: What's Wrong with Humanitarian Aid?* (New York: Henry Holt, 2010), p. 153.

78 Nicholas de Torrente, "Humanitarian Action under Attack: Reflections on the Iraq War," Paul O'Brien, "Politicized Humanitarianism: A Response to Nicolas de Torrente," and Kenneth Anderson, "Humanitarian Inviolability in Crisis: The Meaning of Impartiality and Neutrality for UN and NGO Agencies Following the 2003–2004 Afghanistan and Iraq Conflicts," *Harvard Human Rights Journal* 17 (2004): 1–30, 31–40, and 41–74, respectively.

79 Antonio Donini, Larry Minear, Ian Smillie, Ted van Barda, and Anthony C. Welsh, *Mapping the Security Environment: Understanding the Perceptions of Local Communities, Peace Support Operations and Assistance Agencies* (Medford, MA: Feinstein International Famine Center, 2005), p. 60.

80 Laura Hammond, "The Power of Holding Humanitarianism Hostage and the Myth of Protective Principles," in *Humanitarianism in Question: Politics, Power, Ethics*, ed. Michael Barnett and Thomas G. Weiss (Ithaca, NY: Cornell University Press, 2008), p. 173.

81 Jeffrey Gettleman, "Contractors are Accused of Large-scale Theft of Food Aid in Somalia," *New York Times*, August 16, 2011.

82 Marrack Goulding, "The Evolution of United Nations Peacekeeping," *Journal of International Affairs* 69, no. 3 (1993): 457.

83 David Rieff, A Bed for the Night: Humanitarianism in Crisis (New York: Simon & Schuster, 2002), p. 207.

84 David Rieff, At the Point of a Gun: Democratic Dreams and Armed Intervention (New York: Simon & Schuster, 2005).

85 David Rieff, "Afterword," in Humanitarian Negotiations Revealed, ed. Magone et al., p. 251.

86 Sarah Collinson and Samir Elhawary, Humanitarian Space: A Review of Trends and Issues, HPG Report 32 (London: Overseas Development Institute, 2012).

87 Enrique Ballestros, Report on the Question of the Use of Mercenaries as a Means of Violating Human Rights and Impeding the Exercise of the Rights of People to Self-Determination (report to Commission on Human Rights, Geneva, January 13, 1999).

88 Stewart Payne, "Teenagers Used for Sex in Bosnia," Daily Telegraph, April 25, 2002.

89 Jon Boone, "Foreign Contractors Hired Afghan 'Dancing Boys,' WikiLeaks Cable Reveals," Guardian, December 2, 2010, available at: www.guardian.co.uk/world/2010/dec/02/foreign-contractors-hired-dancing-boys (accessed July 17, 2012).

90 Peter J. Hoffman, The New Politics of Protecting Humanitarian Space: A Private Security Revolution in Humanitarian Affairs? unpublished PhD dissertation, The Graduate Center, The City University of New York, 2012.

91 Abby Stoddard, Adele Harmer, and Victoria DiDomenico, The Use of Private Security Providers and Services in Humanitarian Operations, HPG Report 27 (London: Overseas Development Institute, 2008), p. 13.

92 ICRC, "The ICRC to Expand Contracts with Private Military and Security Companies," August 4, 2004, available at: www.icrc.org/eng/resources/documents/misc/63he58.htm (accessed July 17, 2012).

93 Myron Wiener, "The Clash of Norms: Dilemmas in Refugee Policies," in Workshop on the Demography of Forced Migration (Washington, DC: National Academy of Sciences, 1997), p. 5.

94 Hugo Slim, "Idealism and Realism in Humanitarian Action," in Essays In Humanitarian Action (Oxford: Oxford Institute for Ethics, Law, and Armed Conflict, University of Oxford, 2012; Kindle edn).

95 David Kennedy, *The Dark Sides of Virtue: Reassessing International Humanitarianism* (Princeton, NJ: Princeton University Press, 2004).

96 Anderson, *Do No Harm*; Hugo Slim, "Doing the Right Thing: Relief Agencies, Moral Dilemmas, and Moral Responsibility in Political Emergencies and War," *Disasters* 21, no. 3 (1997): 244–57; Duffield, *Global Governance and the New Wars*, pp. 90–5; and Des Gasper, "'Drawing a Line' – Ethical and Political Strategies in Complex Emergency Assistance," *European Journal of Development Research* 11, no. 2 (1999): 87–114.

97 See James D. Fearon, "The Rise of Emergency Relief Aid," in *Humanitarianism in Question*, ed. Barnett and Weiss, pp. 49–72.

98 Ian Smillie and Larry Minear, *The Charity of Nations: Humanitarian Action in a Calculating World* (Bloomfield, CT: Kumarian, 2004), p. 1.

99 Marc Lindenberg and Coralie Bryant, *Going Global: Transforming Relief and Development NGOs* (Bloomfield, CT: Kumarian, 2001), p. 76.

100 Thomas G. Weiss, *Military–Civilian Interactions: Humanitarian Crises and the Responsibility to Protect*, 2nd edn (Lanham, MD: Rowman & Littlefield, 2005), pp. 192–7.

101 Simon Chesterman, *Just Law or Just Peace? Humanitarian Intervention and International Law* (Oxford: Oxford University Press, 2001).

102 Thomas G. Weiss, "RtoP Alive and Well after Libya," *Ethics & International Affairs* 25, no. 3 (2011): 287–92.

103 See Timothy W. Crawford and Alan Kuperman, eds., *Gambling on Humanitarian Intervention: Moral Hazard, Rebellion, and Internal War* (New York: Routledge, 2006). See also Alan J. Kuperman, "Mitigating the Moral Hazard of Humanitarian Intervention: Lessons from Economics," *Global Governance* 14, no. 2 (2008): 219–40; "The Moral Hazard of Humanitarian Intervention: Lessons from the Balkans," *International Studies Quarterly* 52 (2008): 49–80; and "Darfur: Strategic Victimhood Strikes Again?" *Genocide Studies and Prevention* 4, no. 3 (2009): 281–303.

104 For a thoughtful and thorough criticism, see Alexander Bellamy and Paul D. Williams, "On the Limits of Moral Hazard: The Responsibility to Protect, Armed Conflict and Mass Atrocities,"

European Journal of International Relations (May 12, 2011), available at: ejt.sagepub.com/content/early/2011/05/12/1354066 110393366.full.pdf+html (accessed July 17, 2012).

105 Michael Ignatieff, Empire Lite: Nation-Building in Bosnia, Kosovo, and Afghanistan (Toronto: Penguin, 2003), p. 19; and Rieff, A Bed for the Night, p. 191.

106 Duffield, Global Governance and the New Wars, p. 75.

CHAPTER 3 COORDINATION VS. COMPETITION IN AN UNREGULATED MARKET

1 Leon Gordenker, "United Nations System," in Global Governance and International Organization, ed. Thomas G. Weiss and Rorden Wilkinson (London: Routledge, forthcoming).

2 Antonio Donini, "The Evolving Nature of Coordination," in The OCHA, Humanitarian Decade, UN 131, which updates his work The Policies of Mercy: UN Coordination in Afghanistan, Mozambique and Rwanda, Occasional Paper #22 (Providence, RI: Watson Institute, 1996), p. 14.

3 Mario Bettati, Le droit d'ingérence: Mutation de l'ordre international (Paris: Odile Jacob, 1996). Eliasson is now UN deputy secretary-general.

4 Jacques Cuénod, "Coordinating United Nations Humanitarian Assistance," RPG Focus (Washington, DC: RPG, 1993).

5 Kofi Annan, Renewing the United Nations: A Programme for Reform (New York: UN, 1997). For details, see Thomas G. Weiss, "Humanitarian Shell Games: Whither UN Reform?" Security Dialogue 29, no.1 (1998): 9–23.

6 High-level Panel on UN System-wide Coherence on Development, Humanitarian Assistance and the Environment, Delivering as One (New York: UN, 2006); and United Nations, A Capacity Study of the United Nations Development System (Geneva: UN, 1969), 2 volumes, document DP/5.

7 Oxfam, Oxfam Annual Report 2009–10, available at: www.oxfam.org/sites/www.oxfam.org/files/oxfam-international-annual-report-2009-2010.pdf (accessed July 17, 2012).

8 Stichting Oxfam International, Annual Report and Non-Statutory Financial Statements For the Year Ended 31 March 2011, available at: www.oxfam.org/sites/www.oxfam.org/files/

stichting-oxfam-international-financial-accounts-2010-11.pdf
(accessed July 17, 2012).

9 CARE International, CARE International Annual Report 2010,
available at: www.care-international.org/Annual-Report/annual-
report.html (accessed July 17, 2012).

10 Médecins sans Frontières, MSF Financial Report 2010,
available at: www.msf.org/msf/articles/2011/07/msf-financial-
report-2010.cfm (accessed July 17, 2012).

11 Save the Children International, *Becoming One: Save the Children
Annual Review 2010* (London: Save the Children, 2011).

12 World Vision, Consolidated Financial Statements: World
Vision, Inc. and Affiliates (With Independent Auditors' Report
Thereon), September 30, 2009 and 2010, available at: www.
worldvision.org/resources.nsf/Main/annual-review-2010-
resources/$FILE/AR_2010AuditedFinancialStatement.pdf
(accessed July 17, 2012).

13 The American Council for Voluntary International Action,
Financial Statements, American Council for Voluntary
International Action, for the Years Ended December 31, 2010
and 2009, available at: www.interaction.org/sites/default/
files/2190/2010-990.pdf (accessed July 17, 2012).

14 VOICE, Activity Report 2010, available at: www.ngovoice.org/
documents/activity%20report%20FINAL-for%20website.pdf
(accessed July 17, 2012).

15 James D. Fearon, "The Rise of Emergency Relief Aid," in
Humanitarianism in Question: Politics, Power, Ethics, ed. Michael
Barnett and Thomas G. Weiss (Ithaca, NY: Cornell University
Press, 2008), pp. 67–8.

16 Abby Stoddard, Adele Harmer, and Katherine Haver, *Providing
Aid in Insecure Environments: Trends in Policy and Operations*, HPG
Report 23 (London: Overseas Development Institute, 2006), p. 16.

17 See Abdel-Rahman Ghandour, *Jihad humanitaire* (Paris:
Flammarion, 2002).

18 Michael Fullilove, *World Wide Webs: Diasporas and the
International System* (Sydney: Lowy Institute for International
Policy, 2009).

19 Fabrice Weissman, "Introduction," in *In the Shadow of "Just
Wars": Violence, Politics, and Humanitarian Action*, ed. Fabrice
Weissman (Ithaca, NY: Cornell University Press, 2004), p. 12.

20 Alexander Cooley and James Ron, "The NGO Scramble:

Organizational Insecurity and the Political Economy of Transnational Action," *International Security* 27, no. 1 (2002): 6.

21 Mancur Olson, *The Logic of Collective Action: Public Goods and the Theory of Groups* (Cambridge, MA: Harvard University Press, 1965).

22 Alex de Waal, *Famine Crimes: Politics and the Humanitarian Relief Industry in Africa* (Oxford: James Currey, 1997), pp. 64–5.

23 Max P. Glaser, "Humanitarian Engagement with Nonstate Armed Actors," *The Parameters of Negotiated Access*, HPN Network Paper 51 (June 2005), pp. 5 and 17; and UN Security Council document S/2001/331/, especially paras. 14–16.

24 Michael Maren, *The Road to Hell: The Ravaging Effects of Foreign Aid and International Charity* (New York: Free Press, 1997), p. 219.

25 "Tsunami: Learning from the Humanitarian Responses," special issue of *Forced Migration Review*, July 2005.

26 Anne Vallaeys, *Médecins Sans Frontières: La Biographie* (Paris: Fayort, 2004); and Stephen Hopgood, *Keepers of the Flame: Understanding Amnesty International* (Ithaca, NY: Cornell University Press, 2006).

27 David Rieff, *A Bed for the Night: Humanitarianism in Crisis* (New York: Simon & Schuster, 2002), p. 184.

28 Michael Barnett and Janice Gross Stein, eds., *Sacred Aid: Faith and Humanitarianism* (Oxford: Oxford University Press, 2012).

29 Hugo Slim, "Idealism and Realism in Humanitarian Action," in *Essays In Humanitarian Action* (Oxford: Oxford Institute for Ethics, Law, and Armed Conflict, University of Oxford, 2012; Kindle edn).

30 Cooley and Ron, "The NGO Scramble," p. 13.

31 The original title of the book published in English as Claire Magone, Michael Neuman, and Fabrice Weissman, eds., *Humanitarian Negotiations Revealed: The MSF Experience* (London: Hurst, 2012).

CHAPTER 4 MARKET DISTORTIONS FROM ABOVE AND BELOW

1 Laura Hammond, "The Power of Holding Humanitarianism Hostage and the Myth of Protective Principles," in

Humanitarianism in Question: Politics, Power, Ethics, ed. Michael Barnett and Thomas G. Weiss (Ithaca, NY: Cornell University Press, 2008), pp. 172–95.

2   Michael Barnett and Jack Snyder, "The Grand Strategies of Humanitarianism," in *Humanitarianism in Question*, ed. Barnett and Weiss, pp. 143–71.

3   Judith Randel and Tony German, "Trends in Financing of Humanitarian Assistance," in *The New Humanitarianisms: A Review of Trends in Global Humanitarian Action*, ed. Joanna Macrae (London: Overseas Development Institute, 2002), p. 21.

4   Global Humanitarian Assistance, "03/Global Humanitarian Assistance," in *GHA Report 2009* (Wells, UK: Development Initiatives, 2009), p. 8, available at: www.globalhumanitarian assistance.org/reports (accessed July 18, 2012).

5   Ian Smillie, *The Emperor's Old Clothes*, unpublished manuscript, Feinstein Center, Tufts University, n.d., p.1.

6   Randel and German, "Trends in Financing of Humanitarian Assistance," p. 27.

7   Ian Smillie and Larry Minear, *The Charity of Nations: Humanitarian Action in a Calculating World* (Bloomfield, CT: Kumarian, 2004), p. 145; and Oxfam, *Beyond the Headlines: An Agenda for Action to Protect Civilians in Neglected Countries* (Oxford: Oxfam International, 2003), p. 2.

8   OCHA, *Chapeau of the Mid-Year Review of the Humanitarian Appeal for 2011* (Geneva: UN, 2011), p. 13.

9   See Virginia Gamba and Richard Cronwell, "Arms, Elites, and Resources in the Angolan Civil War," in *Greed and Grievance: Economic Agendas in Civil Wars*, ed. Mats Berdal and David M. Malone (Boulder, CO: Lynne Rienner Publishers, 2000), pp. 157–72.

10 Dwight D. Eisenhower, "Farewell Address," 1961, reprinted in *A Documentary History of the United States*, ed. Richard D. Heffner (New York: Mentor, 1976), p. 314.

11 Mark Duffield, "Globalization, Transborder Trade, and War Economies," in *Greed and Grievance*, ed. Berdal and Malone, pp. 72–3.

12 Beatrice Hibou, "The 'Social Capital' of the State as an Agent of Deception," in *The Criminalization of the State in Africa*, ed. Jean-François Bayart, Stephen Ellis, and Beatrice Hibou (Bloomington: Indiana University Press, 1999), pp. 71, 96.

13 Phil Williams, "Transnational Organized Crime and the State,"
    in *The Emergence of Private Authority in Global Governance*, ed.
    Rodney Bruce Hall and Thomas J. Biersteker (Cambridge:
    Cambridge University Press, 2002), pp. 161–82; Louis Shelly,
    "Transnational Organized Crime: An Imminent Threat to the
    Nation-State," *Journal of International Affairs* 48, no. 2 (Winter
    1995): 464–89; and Phil Williams, "Transnational Criminal
    Organizations and International Security," *Survival* 36, no. 1
    (1994): 96–113.
14 Michael Klare, *Resource Wars: The New Landscape of Global
    Conflict* (New York: Henry Holt, 2002).
15 Indra de Soysa, "Resource Curse: Are Civil Wars Driven
    by Rapacity or Paucity," in *Greed and Grievance*, ed. Berdal
    and Malone, pp. 113–35. Also see Richard M. Auty, *Resource
    Abundance and Economic Development* (Oxford: Oxford University
    Press, 2001).
16 David Keen, *The Economic Functions of Violence in Civil Wars*
    (Oxford: Oxford University Press, 1998); Berdal and Malone,
    eds., *Greed and Grievance*; and Mark Duffield, *Global Governance
    and the New Wars: The Merging of Development and Security*
    (London: Zed, 2001), pp. 161–201.
17 Paul Collier, "Economic Causes of Conflict and Their
    Implications for Policy," World Bank paper dated June 15, 2000;
    and Paul Collier and Nicholas Sambanis, "Understanding Civil
    War: A New Agenda," *Journal of Conflict Resolution* 46, no. 1
    (2002): 3–12.
18 Global Witness reported that "oil production . . . exacerbated
    social inequalities in Angola, basically benefiting only a very
    small elite and sustaining the war effort." See Global Witness,
    "A Crude Awakening: The Role of the Oil and Banking
    Industries in Angola's Civil War and the Plunder of State
    Assets," December 1999, available at: www.globalwitness.org/
    library/crude-awakening (accessed July 18, 2012).
19 Klare, *Resource Wars*, p. 192.
20 Human Rights Watch, "Nigeria: No Democratic Dividend,"
    October 2002, available at: www.hrw.org/news/2002/10/22/
    nigeria-no-democratic-dividend-oil-delta (accessed July 18, 2012).
21 Chantal de Jonge Oudraat, "Intervention: Trends and
    Challenges," in *New Millennium, New Perspectives: The United
    Nations, Security, and Governance*, ed. Ramesh Thakur and

Edward Newman (Tokyo and New York: United Nations
University Press, 2000), p. 62. See also James Rupert,
"Diamond Hunters Fuel Africa's Brutal Wars," *Washington Post*,
October 16, 1999.

22　See R.T. Naylor, *Economic Warfare: Sanctions, Embargo Busting,
and Their Human Cost* (Boston: Northeastern University Press,
2001).

23　Karen Ballentine and Jake Sherman, "Introduction," in *The
Political Economy of Armed Conflict: Beyond Greed and Grievance*,
ed. Karen Ballentine and Jack Sherman (Boulder, CO: Lynne
Rienner Publishers, 2003), p. 1.

24　Thomas G. Weiss and Peter J. Hoffman, "Making
Humanitarianism Work," in *Making States Work: State Failure
and the Crisis of Governance*, ed. Simon Chesterman, Michael
Ignatieff, and Ramesh Thakur (Tokyo: UN University Press,
2005), pp. 296–317.

25　United Nations, *Programme of Action to Prevent, Combat, and
Eradicate the Illicit Trade in Small Arms and Light Weapons in All
Its Aspects*, UN document A/CONF.192/1.5, July 20, 2001; and
Keith Krause, "Multilateral Diplomacy, Norm Building, and UN
Conferences: The Case of Small Arms and Light Weapons,"
Global Governance 8, no. 2 (2002): 247–63.

26　United Nations, *The Causes of Conflict and the Promotion of
Durable Peace and Sustainable Development in Africa*, report of the
UN secretary-general to the Security Council, April 1998.

27　Global Witness, www.globalwitness.org/campaigns/diamonds
(accessed July 18, 2012). The UN is also engaged in action to
clean up the diamond trade, see www.un.org/peace/africa/
Diamond.html (accessed July 18, 2012).

28　"Diamond Development Initiative Begins: New Approach to
Africa's Diamond Problems," August 17, 2005, available at:
www.globalwitness.org/library/diamond-development-initiative-
begins (accessed July 18, 2012). Global Witness, "Why We Are
Leaving the Kimberley Process," December 5, 2011, available at:
www.globalwitness.org/library/why-we-are-leaving-kimberley-
process-message-global-witness-founding-director-charmian-
gooch (accessed July 19, 2012).

29　Stephen John Stedman, "Spoiler Problems in Peace Processes,"
in *Nationalism and Ethnic Conflict*, ed. Michael E. Brown,
Owen R. Coté, Jr., Sean M. Lynn-Jones, and Steven E. Miller

(Cambridge, MA: MIT Press, 2001), pp. 366–414, and "Introduction" and "Policy Implications," in *Ending Civil Wars: The Implementation of Peace Agreements*, ed. Stephen John Stedman, Donald Rothchild, and Elizabeth M. Cousens (Boulder, CO: Lynne Rienner Publishers, 2002), pp. 1–40 and 663–71.

30 Fiona Terry, *Condemned to Repeat? The Paradox of Humanitarian Action* (Ithaca, NY: Cornell University Press, 2002), p. 44.

31 Larry Minear in collaboration with Tabviegen Agnes Abuom, Eshetu Chole, Kosti Maribe, Aboul Mohammed, Jennefer Sebstad, and Thomas G. Weiss, *Humanitarianism under Siege: A Critical Review of Operation Lifeline Sudan* (Trenton, NJ: Red Sea Press, 1991); and Francis M. Deng and Larry Minear, *The Challenge of Famine Relief: Emergency Operations in the Sudan* (Washington, DC: Brookings Institution, 1992).

32 See Susan Woodward, *Balkan Tragedy: Chaos and Dissolution after the Cold War* (Washington, DC: Brookings Institution, 1995); and Nicholas Morris, "Humanitarian Aid and Neutrality," paper presented at the Conference on the Promotion and Protection of Human Rights in Acute Crisis, London, February 1998, available at: www.essex.ac.uk/rightsinacutecrisis/report/morris.htm (accessed July 18, 2012).

33 Linda Polman, *The Crisis Caravan: What's Wrong with Humanitarian Aid?* (New York: Henry Holt, 2010), pp. 96–9.

34 Ilene Cohn and Guy S. Goodwin-Gill, *Child Soldiers: The Role of Children in Armed Conflict* (Oxford: Clarendon Press, 1994); and Graça Machel, *The Impact of War on Children* (New York: Palgrave, 2001).

35 Mark Duffield, "The Political Economy of Internal War: Asset Transfer, Complex Emergencies and International Aid," in *War and Hunger: Rethinking International Responses to Complex Emergencies*, ed. Joanna Macrae and Anthony Zwi (London: Zed, 1994), pp. 56–57; and David Keen and Ken Wilson, "Engaging with Violence: A Reassessment of Relief in Wartime," in *War and Hunger*, ed. Macrae and Zwi, p. 217.

36 Andrew S. Natsios, "Humanitarian Relief Intervention in Somalia: The Economics in Chaos," *International Peacekeeping* 3, no. 1 (1996): 68–91.

37 For instance, Alex de Waal, *Famine Crimes: Politics and the Disaster Relief Industry in Africa* (Oxford: James Currey, 1997); William

Shawcross, *Deliver Us from Evil: Peacekeepers, Warlords, and a World of Endless Conflict* (New York: Simon & Schuster, 2000); and Michael Maren, *The Road to Hell: The Ravaging Effects of Foreign Aid and International Charity* (New York: Free Press, 1997).

38 Duffield, *Global Governance and the New Wars*; and *Aid Policy and Post-modern Conflict: A Critical Review*, Occasional Paper 19 (Birmingham, UK: School of Public Policy, 1998). See also Graham Hancock, *Lords of Poverty: The Power, Prestige, and Corruption of the International Aid Business* (New York: Monthly Review Press, 1992).

39 Tony Vaux, *The Selfish Altruist: Relief Work in Famine and War* (London, Earthscan, 2001).

40 Mary B. Anderson and Peter J. Woodrow, *Rising from the Ashes: Development Strategies in Times of Disaster* (Boulder, CO: Westview, 1987); and Mary B. Anderson, *Do No Harm: How Aid Can Support Peace – or War* (Boulder, CO: Lynne Rienner Publishers, 1999).

41 Jan Egeland, Adele Harmer, and Abby Stoddard, *To Stay and Deliver: Good Practice for Humanitarians in Complex Security Environments* (New York: OCHA, 2011), p. viii.

42 'USAID Administrator: "NGOs Must Promote Ties to US Government or We Will 'Find New Partners'," 'available at: www.worldhunger.org/articles/03/us/natsiosinteraction.htm (accessed July 18, 2012).

43 Quoted in Smillie and Minear, *The Charity of Nations*, p. 143.

44 Marie-Pierre Allié, "Acting at Any Price?" in *Humanitarian Negotiations Revealed: The MSF Experience*, ed. Claire Magone, Michael Neuman, and Fabrice Weissman (London: Hurst, 2012), p. 3.

45 Adele Harmer, Lin Cotterrell, and Abby Stoddard, *From Stockholm to Ottawa: A Progress Review of the Good Humanitarian Donorship Initiative*, HPG Research Briefing 18 (London: Overseas Development Institute, 2004).

CHAPTER 5 THE PUSH AND PULL OF COMING TO THE RESCUE

1 Michael Ignatieff, "Intervention and State Failure," in *The New Killing Fields: Massacre and the Politics of Intervention*, ed.

Nicolaus Mills and Kira Brunner (New York: Basic Books, 2002), pp. 229–44.

2 Michael Barnett, "The New United Nations Politics of Peace: From Juridical Sovereignty to Empirical Sovereignty," *Global Governance* 1, no. 1 (1995): 79–97.

3 Secretary of State Colin Powell, Remarks to the National Foreign Policy Conference for Leaders of Nongovernmental Organizations, Washington, DC, October 26, 2001, available at: avalon.law.yale.edu/sept11/powell_brief31.asp (accessed July 19, 2012).

4 Antonio Donini, "The Evolving Nature of Coordination," in *The Humanitarian Decade: Challenges for Humanitarian Assistance in the Last Decade and into the Future*, Vol. 2, ed. OCHA (New York: UN, 2004), p. 136.

5 Sara Pantuliano, Kate Mackintosh, and Samir Elhawary with Victoria Metcalfe, "Counter-Terrorism and Humanitarian Action," HPG Brief 43 (London: Overseas Development Institute, 2011).

6 Save the Children, *Provincial Reconstruction Teams and Humanitarian–Military Relations in Afghanistan* (London: Save the Children, 2004), 5, available at: www.savethechildren.org.uk/sites/default/files/docs/Provincial_Reconstruction_Teams_and_Humanitarian-Military_Relations_in_Afghanistan_2004_09_1.pdf (accessed July 19, 2012).

7 UNHCR, *The State of the World's Refugees 2012: In Search of Solidarity* (Oxford: Oxford University Press, 2012), p. 23.

8 Kofi Annan, "Note from the Secretary-General, Guidance on Integrated Missions," dated 9 February 2006.

9 UNHCR, *The State of the World's Refugees 2012*, p. 24.

10 Quoted by Samantha Power, *A Problem from Hell: America and the Age of Genocide* (New York: Basic Books, 2002), p. 12.

11 Sadako Ogata, *The Turbulent Decade: Confronting the Refugee Crises of the 1990s* (New York: Norton, 2005), p. 25.

12 Mark Duffield, *Global Governance and the New Wars: The Merging of Development and Security* (London: Zed, 2001), pp. 109–13.

13 Alex de Waal, *Famine Crimes: Politics and the Disaster Relief Industry in Africa* (Oxford: James Currey, 1997), p. 221.

14 Global Humanitarian Assistance, *GHA Report 2011* (Wells, UK: Development Initiatives, 2011), p. 50, available at: www.

globalhumanitarianassistance.org/reports (accessed July 18, 2012).

15 International Commission on Intervention and State Sovereignty, *The Responsibility to Protect* (Ottawa: International Development Research Centre, 2001); and Thomas G. Weiss and Don Hubert, *The Responsibility to Protect: Research, Bibliography, Background* (Ottawa: International Development Research Centre, 2001). For interpretations by commissioners, see Gareth Evans, *The Responsibility to Protect: Ending Mass Atrocity Crimes Once and for All* (Washington, DC: Brookings Institution, 2008); and Ramesh Thakur, *The United Nations, Peace and Security: From Collective Security to the Responsibility to Protect* (Cambridge: Cambridge University Press, 2006). The author's version is *Humanitarian Intervention: Ideas in Action*, 2nd edn (Cambridge: Polity Press, 2012).

16 *2005 World Summit Outcome*, UN General Assembly Resolution A/RES/60/1, 24 October 2005, paras. 138–40.

17 Nicholas J. Wheeler, *Saving Strangers: Humanitarian Intervention in International Society* (Oxford: Oxford University Press, 2000).

18 Evans, *The Responsibility to Protect*, p. 28.

19 Edward C. Luck, "The Responsibility to Protect: The First Decade," *Global Responsibility to Protect* 3, no. 4 (2011): 387–99.

20 High-level Panel on Threats, Challenges and Change, *A More Secure World: Our Shared Responsibility* (New York: UN, 2004), para. 203.

21 Kofi A. Annan, *In Larger Freedom: Towards Development, Security and Human Rights for All* (New York: UN, 2005).

22 Edward C. Luck, "The United Nations and the Responsibility to Protect," *Policy Analysis Brief* (Muscatine, IA: Stanley Foundation, 2008), p. 8.

23 Ban Ki-moon, "On Responsible Sovereignty: International Cooperation for a Changed World," Address of the Secretary-General, Berlin, 15 July 2008, UN document SG/SM/11701.

24 Anna Jeffreys, "Giving Voice to Silent Emergencies," April 3, 2002, available at: www.odihpn.org/humanitarian-exchange-magazine/issue-20/giving-voice-to-silent-emergencies (accessed July 19, 2012).

25 International Federation of Red Cross and Red Crescent Societies, *World Disasters Report 2003: Focus on Ethics in Aid* (Bloomfield, CT: Kumarian, 2003), pp. 19–22.

26 Toby Porter, "The Partiality of Humanitarian Assistance
    – Kosovo in Comparative Perspective," *The Journal of
    Humanitarian Assistance* (June 2000): 7, available at: sites.tufts.
    edu/jha/archives/150 (accessed July 19, 2012).
27 See UN OCHA, Consolidated Appeal Process, available at: www.
    unocha.org/cap/ (accessed July 19, 2012).
28 Quoted by Linda Polman, *The Crisis Caravan: What's Wrong with
    Humanitarian Aid?* (New York: Henry Holt, 2010), p. 158.

CHAPTER 6 WHAT NEXT?

1 Adam B. Siegel, "Civil–Military Marriage Counseling: Can This
    Union Be Saved?" *Special Warfare* (December 2002): 28.
2 Arthur C. Helton, "Rescuing the Refugees," *Foreign Affairs*
    81, no. 2 (2002): 72; and *The Price of Indifference: Refugees
    and Humanitarian Action in the New Century* (Oxford: Oxford
    University Press, 2002).
3 Global Humanitarian Assistance, *GHA Report 2011* (Wells,
    UK: Development Initiatives, 2011), p. 61, available at: www.
    globalhumanitarianassistance.org/reports (accessed July 18,
    2012).
4 Global Humanitarian Assistance, "01/Executive Summary," in
    GHA Report 2009 (Wells, UK: Development Initiatives, 2009),
    p. 4, available at: www.globalhumanitarianassistance.org/reports
    (accessed July 18, 2012).
5 Global Humanitarian Assistance, *GHA Report 2011*, p. 2.
6 Ibid., p. 44.
7 See Thomas G. Weiss and David A. Korn, *Internal Displacement:
    Conceptualization and Its Consequences* (London: Routledge,
    2006).
8 Interview with the author, October 11, 2005.
9 Abby Stoddard, Adele Harmer, Katherine Haver, Dirk
    Salomons, and Victoria Wheeler, *Cluster Approach Evaluation
    Final Draft* (New York: OCHA Evaluation and Studies Section,
    2007), p. 1.
10 UNHCR, *The State of the World's Refugees 2012: In Search of
    Solidarity* (Oxford: Oxford University Press, 2012), p. 128.
11 Linda Polman, *The Crisis Caravan: What's Wrong with
    Humanitarian Aid?* (New York: Henry Holt, 2010), p. 176.

12 The Secretary-General's Five-year Action Agenda, 25 January
    2012, available at: www.un.org/sg/priorities/secure_world.shtml
    (accessed July 20, 2012).
13 Janice Gross Stein, "Humanitarian Organizations: Accountable
    – Why, to Whom, for What, and How?" in *Humanitarianism in
    Question: Politics, Power, Ethics*, ed. Michael Barnett and Thomas
    G. Weiss (Ithaca, NY: Cornell University Press, 2008), p. 124.
14 Janice Gross Stein, "Humanitarianism as Political Fusion,"
    Perspectives on Politics 3, no. 4 (2005): 741.
15 See David Loquercio, Mark Hammersley, and Ben Emmens,
    *Understanding and Addressing Staff Turnover in Humanitarian
    Agencies*, HPN Number 55 (London: Overseas Development
    Institute, 2006), p. 5; and David Loquercio, "Turnover and
    Retention: Literature Review for People in Aid," January 2006,
    p. 4, available at: www.peopleinaid.org/pool/files/pubs/turnover-
    and-retention-lit-review-summary-jan-2006.pdf (accessed July
    20, 2012).
16 Stein, "Humanitarian Organizations," p. 141.
17 World Bank, *World Development Report 2011: Conflict, Security,
    and Development* (Washington, DC: World Bank, 2011), p. 31.
18 Stein, "Humanitarian Organizations," p. 142.
19 Global Humanitarian Assistance, *GHA Report 2011*, pp. 64–5.
20 Steven Holloway, "US Unilateralism at the UN: Why Great
    Powers Do Not Make Great Multilateralists," *Global Governance*
    6, no. 3 (2000): 361–81.
21 Jarat Chopra and Thomas G. Weiss, "Prospects for Containing
    Conflict in the Former Second World," *Security Studies* 4,
    no. 3 (1995): 552–83; and Thomas G. Weiss, ed., *Beyond UN
    Subcontracting: Task-sharing with Regional Security Arrangements
    and Service-providing NGOs* (London: Macmillan, 1997).
22 Peter Walker and Catherine Russ, *Professionalizing the
    Humanitarian Sector: A Scoping Study*, report commissioned by
    Enhancing Learning & Research for Humanitarian Assistance,
    April 2010.
23 Joshua S. Goldstein, *Winning the War on War: The Decline of
    Armed Conflict Worldwide* (New York: Dutton, 2011), p. 272.
24 David Rieff, "Millions May Die . . . Or Not," *Foreign Policy*
    (September/October 2011): 22–4.
25 Global Humanitarian Assistance, *GHA Report 2011*, p. 64.
26 This section draws on Peter J. Hoffman and Thomas G. Weiss,

"Humanitarianism and Practitioners," in *Humanitarianism in Question*, ed. Barnett and Weiss, pp. 264–85.

27 Michael Barnett, *Empire of Humanity: A History of Humanitarianism* (Ithaca, NY: Cornell University Press, 2011).

28 Larry Minear, *The Humanitarian Enterprise: Dilemmas and Discoveries* (Bloomfield, CT: Kumarian, 2002), p. 7.

29 Hugo Slim, "Global Welfare: A Realistic Expectation for the International Humanitarian System?" *ALNAP Review of Humanitarian Action in 2005: Evaluation Utilisation* (December 2006), pp. 15 and 30.

30 World Bank, "Main Messages," in *World Development Report 2011: Conflict, Security, and Development* (Washington, DC: World Bank, 2011), p. i.

31 Human Security Report Project, *Human Security Report 2009/10* (New York: Oxford University Press, 2011); and Goldstein, *Winning the War on War*.

32 Thomas G. Weiss, "The Humanitarian Impulse," in *The UN Security Council: From the Cold War to the 21st Century*, ed. David Malone (Boulder, CO: Lynne Rienner, 2004), pp. 37–54.

33 David Rieff, "Afterword," in *Humanitarian Negotiations Revealed: The MSF Experience*, ed. Claire Magone, Michael Neuman, and Fabrice Weissman (London: Hurst, 2012), pp. 251–2.

34 Myron Wiener, "The Clash of Norms: Dilemmas in Refugee Policies," in *Workshop on the Demography of Forces Migration* (Washington, DC: National Academy of Sciences, 1997), p. 5. See also Margaret E. McGuinness, "Legal and Normative Dimensions of the Manipulation of Refugees," in *Refugee Manipulation: War, Politics, and Human Misery*, ed. Stephen John Stedman and Fred Tanner (Washington, DC: Brookings Institution, 2003), pp. 135–66.

35 Dan Smith, "Interventionist Dilemmas and Justice," in *Humanitarian Force*, ed. Anthony McDermott (Oslo: International Peace Research Institute, 1997), pp. 13–39, esp. 29–31.

36 Thomas Nagel, *Moral Questions* (Cambridge: Cambridge University Press, 1991), p. 74.

37 Arthur Helton, *The Price of Indifference: Refugees and Humanitarian Action in the New Century* (Oxford: Oxford University Press, 2002).

38 Jeff Drumtra, "The Year in Review," in *World Refugee Survey 1996* (Washington, DC: U.S. Committee for Refugees, 1996), p. 11.

Suggested Reading

A rich, diverse, and growing literature exists about the nature of humanitarianism and challenges to its core principles. This brief selection highlights recent books that constitute a starting point for additional reading that should be readily available in most college and university libraries; the endnotes for each chapter contain further possibilities for additional research. The exact placement of a book is subjective because many would be relevant for several of the chapters; but they appear once where I believe that they provide the most insights.

For Chapter 1, a thorough treatment of the antecedents of "Responding to Humanitarian Demands" is Michael Barnett, *Empire of Humanity: A History of Humanitarianism* (Ithaca, NY: Cornell University Press, 2011). Other good overviews, with especial reference to principles and many key actors, are Larry Minear, *The Humanitarian Enterprise: Dilemmas and Discoveries* (Bloomfield, CT: Kumarian, 2002); and Michael Ignatieff, *The Warrior's Honor: Ethnic War and the Modern Conscience* (New York: Holt, 1997). Many of the main IGOs and NGOs are the topics for separate books in the Routledge "Global Institutions Series," edited by Thomas G. Weiss and Rorden Wilkinson. Up-to-date annual overviews of international military efforts can be found in Center for International Cooperation, *Annual Review of Global Peace Operations 2011* (Boulder, CO: Lynne Rienner Publishers, 2011).

For Chapter 2, there are numerous sources that unpack "The Contemporary Landscape: Need and Greed." Good places to start reading about the nature of today's wars are Mary Kaldor, *New and Old Wars: Organized Violence in a Global Era* (Stanford, CA: Stanford University Press, 1999); Mark Duffield, *Global Governance and the New Wars: The Merging of Development and Security* (London: Zed, 2001); Mohammed Ayoob, *The Third World Security Predicament: State Making, Regional Conflict, and the International System* (Boulder, CO: Lynne Rienner Publishers, 1995); Mats Berdal and David M. Malone, eds., *Greed and Grievance: Economic Agendas in Civil Wars* (Boulder, CO: Lynne Rienner Publishers, 2000); and Hugo Slim, *Killing Civilians: Method, Madness, and Morality in War* (New York: Columbia University Press, 2007). The nature of the resulting humanitarian challenges is available in Fiona Terry, *Condemned to Repeat? The Paradox of Humanitarian Action* (Ithaca, NY: Cornell University Press, 2002); David Rieff, *A Bed for the Night: Humanitarianism in Crisis* (New York: Simon & Schuster, 2002); Alex de Waal, *Famine Crimes: Politics and the Disaster Relief Industry in Africa* (Oxford: James Currey, 1997); Fabrice Weissman, ed., *In the Shadow of "Just Wars": Violence, Politics, and Humanitarian Action* (Ithaca, NY: Cornell University Press, 2004); and Claire Magone, Michael Neuman, and Fabrice Weissman, eds., *Humanitarian Negotiations Revealed: The MSF Experience* (London: Hurst, 2012). Peter J. Hoffman and Thomas G. Weiss, *Sword and Salve: Confronting New Wars and Humanitarian Crises* (Lanham, MD: Rowman & Littlefield, 2006) provides an overview of the historical, philosophical, legal, and political foundations of war (interstate and intrastate) and traditional and newer varieties of humanitarian action. Michael Byers's *War Law: Understanding International Law and Armed Conflict* (New York: Grove Press, 2005) is a helpful primer in the relevant public international law that examines under what conditions it is appropriate to use military force when diplomacy has failed.

For Chapter 3, "Coordination vs. Competition in an Unregulated Market," virtually all of the books listed for Chapter 2 are relevant. In addition, an overview with a similar analysis is Michael Barnett and Thomas G. Weiss, *Humanitarianism Contested: Where Angels Fear to Tread* (London: Routledge, 2011). The reader might also wish to consult the following: Abby Stoddard, Adele Harmer, and Katherine Haver, *Providing Aid in Insecure Environments: Trends in Policy and Operations*, HPG Report 23 (London: Overseas Development Institute, 2006); Ian Smillie and Larry Minear, *The Charity of Nations: Humanitarian Action in a Calculating World* (Bloomfield, CT: Kumarian, 2004); Marc Lindenberg and Coralie Bryant, *Going Global: Transforming Relief and Development NGOs* (Bloomfield, CT: Kumarian, 2001); and Adele Harmer and Ellen Martin, *Diversity in Donorship: Field Lessons*, HPG Report 30 (London: Overseas Development Institute, 2010).

Because it is such a factor in explaining the contemporary crisis among humanitarians about how they proceed in war zones, it makes sense to make separate suggestions about military interactions that are central to both Chapters 2 and 3. More detailed political analyses of humanitarian interventions can be found in Nicholas J. Wheeler, *Saving Strangers: Humanitarian Intervention in International Society* (Oxford: Oxford University Press, 2000), and more legal insights in Simon Chesterman, *Just War or Just Peace? Humanitarian Intervention and International Law* (Oxford: Oxford University Press, 2001) and Anne Orford, *International Authority and the Responsibility to Protect* (Cambridge: Cambridge University Press, 2011). For the coming together of the military and humanitarians in the post-Cold War era, see Thomas G. Weiss, *Military–Civilian Interactions: Humanitarian Crises and the Responsibility to Protect*, 2nd edn (Lanham, MD: Rowman & Littlefield, 2005), and James Pattison, *Humanitarian*

Intervention and the Responsibility to Protect (Oxford: Oxford University Press, 2010). For an overview of changing attitudes, see Martha Finnemore, *The Purpose of Intervention: Changing Beliefs about the Use of Military Force* (Ithaca, NY: Cornell University Press, 2003). For case studies of various types of humanitarian military action (logistics, protection of operations and populations, and defeat of perpetrators of violence), see Taylor Seybolt, *Humanitarian Military Operations: Conditions for Success and Failure* (Oxford: Oxford University Press, 2007). Two collections of essays on a wide range of related topics are Jennifer Welsh, ed., *Humanitarian Intervention and International Relations* (Oxford: Oxford University Press, 2004), and J.L. Holzgrefe and Robert O. Keohane, eds., *Humanitarian Intervention: Ethical, Legal, and Political Dilemmas* (Cambridge: Cambridge University Press, 2003).

For Chapter 4 on "Market Distortions from Above and Below," many of the books listed for the previous two chapters also contain insights about the nature of local economies and the range of reactions by humanitarians. In addition, the reader may wish to consult: Michael Maren, *The Road to Hell: The Ravaging Effects of Foreign Aid and International Charity* (New York: Free Press, 1997); Linda Polman, *The Crisis Caravan: What's Wrong with Humanitarian Aid?* (New York: Henry Holt, 2010); and Rachel McCleary, *Global Compassion: Private Voluntary Organizations and US Foreign Policy since 1939* (Oxford: Oxford University Press, 2009). Studies that examine the parameters of the people working in today's war zones are Peter Walker and Catherine Russ, *Professionalizing the Humanitarian Sector: A Scoping Study*, report commissioned by Enhancing Learning & Research for Humanitarian Assistance, April 2010; Chandra Lekha Sriram, John C. King, Julie A. Mertus, Olga Martin-Ortega, and Johanna Herman, eds., *Surviving Field Research: Working* in Violent and Difficult Situations (London: Routledge, 2009); and Cate Buchanan and Robert Muggah, No Relief: Surveying the Effects of Gun Violence on Humanitarian and Development Personnel (Geneva: Centre for Humanitarian Dialogue, 2005). For Chapter 5, "The Push and Pull of Coming to the Rescue," the basic political story of the infringement upon state sovereignty begins with the International Commission on Intervention and State Sovereignty, The Responsibility to Protect (Ottawa: International Development Research Centre, 2001); and Thomas G. Weiss and Don Hubert, The Responsibility to Protect: Research, Bibliography, Background (Ottawa: International Development Research Centre, 2001). Secondary sources include: Gareth Evans, The Responsibility to Protect: Ending Mass Atrocity Crimes Once and for All (Washington, DC: Brookings Institution, 2008); Ramesh Thakur, The United Nations, Peace and Security: From Collective Security to the Responsibility to Protect (Cambridge: Cambridge University Press, 2006); Alex J. Bellamy, Responsibility to Protect: The Global Effort to End Mass Atrocities (Cambridge: Polity Press, 2009); and Thomas G. Weiss, Humanitarian Intervention: Ideas in Action, 2nd edn (Cambridge: Polity Press, 2012). In addition, since 2009, the academic journal Global Responsibility to Protect has been published quarterly. An authoritative and up-to-date analysis of issues and statistics is UNHCR, The State of the World's Refugees 2012: In Search of Solidarity (Oxford: Oxford University Press, 2012).

For Chapter 6, "What Next?" a good place to start is Jonathan Moore, ed., Hard Choices: Moral Dilemmas in Humanitarian Intervention (Lanham, MD: Rowman & Littlefield, 1998). Regarding consolidation, the reader should refer to Antonio Donini, The Policies of Mercy: UN Coordination in Afghanistan, Mozambique, and Rwanda (Providence, RI: Watson Institute, 1996), occasional paper #22. For accountability, a place to begin is Peter Walker and Daniel G. Maxwell, Shaping the

Humanitarian World (London: Routledge, 2009). Finally, for enhanced professionalism and the challenges of applied social science for humanitarian action, the reader should consult a wide-ranging collection of essays, Michael Barnett and Thomas G. Weiss, eds., *Humanitarianism in Question: Politics, Power, Ethics* (Ithaca, NY: Cornell University Press, 2008).

Index

`